Journal of Early Childhood and Infant Psychology

Volume 1

2005

PACE UNIVERSITY PRESS   NEW YORK

ISSN 1554-6144
ISBN 0-944473-72-5

Address Subscription Inquiries to:

Pace University Press
41 Park Row, Room 1510
New York NY 10038

www.pace.edu/press
(212) 346-1405

Journal of Early Childhood and Infant Psychology

Editor

Barbara A. Mowder

Pace University-New York City

Associate Editors

Florence Rubinson
Brooklyn College of the City University of New York

K. Mark Sossin
Pace University-New York City

Anastasia Yasik
Pace University-New York City

Editorial Review Board

Phyllis Ackman
Pace University-New York City

Vincent C. Alfonso
Fordham University

Stephen J. Bagnato
University of Pittsburgh

Anni Bergman
New York University

Zeynep Biringen
Colorado State University

Susan Chinitz
Albert Einstein College of Medicine

Gerard Costa
Youth Consultation Service Institute
for Infant & Preschool Mental Health

Grace Elizalde-Utnick
Brooklyn College of
the City University of New York

Gilbert M. Foley
Yeshiva University

Nancy Evangelista
Alfred University

Madeline Fernandez
Pace University-New
York City

Paul C. McCabe
Brooklyn College of the
City University of New York

Gail Ross
New York Presbyterian Hospital

Mark D. Terjesen
St. John's University

Susan Vig
Children's Evaluation and
Rehabilitation Center

Serena Wieder
Silver Spring, Md.

Editorial Assistants
Rochelle Lebovitch and Elyssa Sperber

Editorial Policy: The Journal of Early Childhood and Infant Psychology (JECIP) is a publication of the New York Association of Early Childhood and Infant Psychologists (NYAECIP). One aspect of NYAECIP's mission is to provide a vehicle for networking within early childhood and infant psychology, including fostering research, scholarship, and professional interactions. This journal (JECIP) focuses on publishing original contributions from a broad range of psychological perspectives relevant to infants, young children, parents, and caregivers. Manuscripts incorporating research, theory and applications within clinical, community, developmental, neurological, and school psychology perspectives are considered. In addition to databased research, the journal accepts test and book reviews, position statements, literature reviews, program descriptions and evaluations, clinical studies, and other professional materials of interest to psychologists working with infants, young children, parents, families, and caregivers.

Format: Manuscripts should be original work not currently submitted for publication to other journals. Authors must follow the guidelines of the *Publication Manual* of the American Psychological Association (Fifth Edition), and not exceed 30 pages including charts, tables, and references.

Submission: Submit five (5) copies and one (1) floppy disk of the manuscript for editorial review. Avoid including any identifying author information in the text. Selection of manuscripts is based on blind peer review. Include a cover page with the following information: the title of article, author(s) full name(s), title(s), institution or professional affiliations, and mailing and email address of primary author. The cover page will not be sent to reviewers.

Selection Criteria:
· Importance of topic in early childhood and infant psychology
· Accuracy and validity of content
· Contribution to professional practice in early childhood and infant psychology
· Clear and concise writing

Submit manuscripts to the Editor at the following address:
Professor Barbara A. Mowder
Editor, JECIP
Psychology Department, Pace University
41 Park Row
New York, New York 10038

Journal of
Early
Childhood and
Infant
Psychology

Volume 1, 2005

New York Association of Early Childhood and Infant Psychologists (NYAECIP): Background, History, and Current Status

Barbara A. Mowder
Pace University-New York City

Florence Rubinson
Brooklyn College

This article provides the background and history of the New York Association of Early Childhood and Infant Psychologists (NYAE-CIP). NYAECIP began in 1997 when a group of psychologists from the New York City area met at Pace University to discuss creating an organization dedicated to furthering practice, research, and policy related to the psychology of young children. In addition, the founding members wanted to establish a vehicle for communication among psychologists interested in infants and young children. Subsequently, NYAECIP leaders and members went on to engage in a variety of professional activities associated with the organization's stated goals. Approximately three times a year NYAECIP sponsors professional meetings where experts present on matters of interest to early childhood and infant psychologists. Recently, NYAECIP has sponsored a number of research projects to delineate the background, role and function, professional activities and materials, and continuing education needs of early childhood and infant certified school psychologists and licensed psychologists throughout New York State. The most recent activity is the creation of the *Journal of Early Childhood and Infant Psychology (JECIP)*.

The New York Association of Early Childhood and Infant Psychologists (NYAECIP) is a professional organization, which was created in 1997. Prior to the creation of this professional organization, a number of New York City psychologists interested in infant and early childhood psychological issues were brought together by Barbara Mowder, Pace University-New York City, to begin discussing the need for a professional group. These early discussions, which occurred in 1996, led to a number of psychologists (e.g., Donna Abel, Vincent Alfonso, Gilbert Foley, Allison Jeffer, Carol Korn, Carol Lidz, Barbara Mowder,

Yvonne Rafferty, Roslyn Ross, Flo Rubinson, Nancee Santandreu, Jay Silverstein, Mark Sossin, Melissa Tarnofsky, and Linda Zaintz) meeting at Pace University-New York City. The group agreed that psychological practice with young children and their families is distinctive from practice with older children. Further, this group posited that the distinctive knowledge base, assessment requirements, competencies and underlying values associated with service delivery to young children are unique. The early NYAECIP participants also maintained that new developments in developmental research, interventions, and pediatric and educational policy demand continuous attention from psychologists to contribute to and remain current in this dynamic area. Therefore, the participants decided to create a group that would address issues associated with this specialty within psychology. Ultimately, in 1997, this group of early childhood and infant psychologists approved by-laws for a new professional organization specifically developed to meet the needs of infant and early childhood psychologists in the New York City area—NYAECIP.

There are many organizations throughout New York State through which members address psychological issues related to young children, but these organizations do so within specific divisions or through time-limited task forces (e.g. New York State Psychological Association, New York Association of School Psychologists, Zero to Three). We know of no professional group that welcomes psychologists with varied training to address solely the burgeoning specialization of infants and young children. With this dearth in mind, the specific purposes of this organization were clearly outlined and appear in the organization's by-laws, including: (a) providing a vehicle for networking within early childhood and infant psychology; fostering research, meetings, writing, and interactions among those interested in early childhood and infant psychology; (b) establishing an identity for early childhood and infant psychology in the New York metropolitan area; (c) working toward the establishment of early childhood and infant psychology as a recognized specialty within our own profession (e.g., APA); (d) acting as a voice for early childhood and infant psychology (e.g., developing policy statements, writing white papers, and advocating for young children, parents, and early childhood and infant psychology); (e) acting as an information and communication vehicle for those interested in early childhood and infant psychology developments, issues, research, and training; and (f) assisting in the development of internship sites for students to develop expertise in early childhood and infant psychology.

During the Spring of NYAECIP's first year, members raised a number of concerns pertaining to early childhood and infant psychology which might be addressed by the group at future meetings, in focus/working groups, or in some other way pertinent to the goals of the organization. The topics raised at the initial meeting, held at Pace University-New York City, included curriculum issues, assessment issues, research issues, treatment issues, and legislative issues. Following adoption of the by-laws, the first NYAECIP meeting was held. The first elected officers were Barbara Mowder as President, Gilbert Foley as President-Elect, Nancee Santandreu as Secretary, Florence Rubinson as Treasurer, and Jay Silverstein as Member-at-Large. Thus, NYAECIP developed in response to needs expressed by early childhood and infant psychologists in the New York City area.

One of the primary activities of NYAECIP has been the presentation of professional workshops and seminars. In accordance with our goal of establishing an identity for psychologists working with young children, the very first presentation, on May 19, 1997, was given by Dr. Carol S. Lidz who was Director of the School Psychology Program at Touro College at that time. The title of her presentation was *Affirming the Role of Psychology in Early Childhood and Infant Psychology*. Following this initial presentation on the role of psychology in the provision of psychological services to young children and their families, a follow-up meeting was planned for the next academic year. On February 6, 1998, Dr. Gil Foley, from Yeshiva University, moved the organization further toward its goal of establishing an identity by presenting a talk entitled, *Psychology: Defining and Affirming Its Identity in Infant and Early Childhood Services*. He, too, spoke to the importance of specially trained psychologists providing services to young children and their families.

The next presentation, on May 15, 1998, took a turn toward policy issues regarding services to young children. The two speakers were Sandra Ginsberg, Assistant Commissioner for Early Intervention Services, with the Department of Mental Health, Mental Retardation, and Alcoholism Services of New York City and Eleanor Greig Ukoli, the Director of Early Childhood and Elementary Education with the New York City Board of Education (now the New York City Department of Education). The topics covered included policy updates on early intervention services in New York City and the new Universal Pre-K initiatives. Later, in 1998, the issue of services to the early childhood bilingual psychological services came to the fore. On October 30, 1998, a number of presenters, including Dr. Emilia Lopez from Queens College, and Dr. Linda Shum from the Herbert G. Birch Early Childhood Center in Riverdale, addressed bilingual issues in providing services to young children and their families. The title of the presentation was *Bilingual Issues in Services to Young Children.*

The issue of bilingual services continued to be a theme for the next NYAECIP meeting on March 5, 1999. Three experts addressed the group in a presentation entitled, *Bilingual Issues in Services to Young Children, Continued.* The presenters included Dr. Graciela Carbajal from Pace University-New York

City, Dr. Graciela Elizalde-Utnick from Brooklyn College, and Dr. Sara Nahari from Queens College. Later that spring, NYAECIP, in an effort to enhance collaborations with other early childhood professionals, held another conference entitled, *Sensory Integration and Update on Universal Pre-K*. Marie Anzalone from the Occupational Therapy Program at Columbia University shared her research as well as insights on collaborations between occupational therapists and psychologists. In addition, Eleanor Greig Ukoli, the Director of Early Childhood and Elementary Education, New York City Board of Education, returned to update members on the progress of Universal Pre-K in New York City.

The next conference returned to the issue of the provision of psychological services to young children and their families. That meeting, held on January 21, 2000, was entitled, *The Role of the Psychologist in Entitling Children to Intervention Services*. The speakers at this meeting included Dr. Vincent Alfonso from Fordham University, Roy Grant from Montefiore Hospital, Dr. Elizabeth Kucera from Mount Sinai Medical Center, and Dr. W. Thomas McMath from Just Kids Diagnostic and Treatment Center in Middle Island, New York. This meeting was followed by a presentation, on June 16, 2000, regarding approaches to treating autism, *Comprehensive Approaches to the Diagnosis and Treatment of Autistic Spectrum Disorders of Relating and Communicating*. Dr. Serena Wieder was scheduled to present, but was unable to at the last moment. In her place, there were a number of presenters presenting diverse points of view regarding services to children with autistic spectrum disorders. More specifically, Dr. Gerald Costa from the Institute for Infant and Preschool Mental Health Training at Youth Consultation Services, Dr. Gil Foley from Yeshiva University, Dr. Andrea Krauss from the Occupational Therapy Program of Touro College, and Dr. Jay Silverstein, the Director of Crossroads Preschool offered and discussed their unique perspectives.

The next presentation by Dr. Phyllis Cohen from the New York Institute for Psychotherapy and Training, and Dr. Phyllis Ackman from the Institute for the Clinical Study of Infants, Toddlers, and Families, on December 15, 2000, turned toward a specific intervention and was entitled, *A Collaborative Treatment Using Videotape Feedback with a Depressed Mother and Her Infant*. On March 16, 2001, Dr. Susan Vig, Director of the Early Intervention Training Institute with the Albert Einstein College of Medicine, offered her perspective on comprehensive assessment with a presentation entitled, *Psychological Assessment of Preschool Children with Developmental Disabilities*. Following this meeting, on June 1, 2001, Dr. Grace Elizalde-Utnick, Brooklyn College, revisited the issue of psychological services to bilingual young children and their families in her talk, *Growing Up with Two Languages: Understanding Childhood Bilingualism and*

Its Implications for Assessment and Learning.

All of the NYAECIP meetings have been held at Pace University-New York City, which is in lower Manhattan, across the street from City Hall and south of the Brooklyn Bridge. On September 11, 2001, there was a horrific tragedy in lower Manhattan, the destruction of the World Trade Center Twin Towers and the death of those who could not escape from the scene. Pace University-New York City is three blocks from the World Trade Center site and the closest center for higher education in the area. The University was closed down for a significant period of time and, when re-opened, was part of the recovery effort. As soon after the tragedy as possible, NYAECIP responded and provided a presentation related to the events of 9/11. On November 16, 2001 NYAECIP offered the presentation, *Helping Young Children and Families Cope with Trauma.* Two renowned specialists on trauma, Dr. Joy Osofsky, and her spouse, Dr. Howard Osofsky, from Louisiana State University Health Sciences Center, spoke to a large assemblage of psychologists and others interested in trauma and young children.

Subsequent to 9/11, NYAECIP offered more presentations. On April 5, 2002, there were a number of presenters speaking on *Psychology in Early Childhood Education and Care.* More specifically, Susan Paula, Director of the Community Support Program at the Children's Hospital at Montefiore and Children's Health Fund, Roy Grant, the Director of Research and Evaluation at the Children's Hospital at Montefiore, Dr. Barbara Mowder, Director of Graduate Psychology Programs at Pace University, and Dr. Florence Rubinson, from the Graduate Program in School Psychology at Brooklyn College were the presenters. Each presenter spoke on a different topic related to providing psychological services within the early childhood arena.

One year after 9/11, NYAECIP continued focusing on issues related to children and trauma. On November 1, 2002, Dr. Susan Paula, from the Children's Health Fund and the Children's Hospital at Montefiore, presented *The Role of the Psychologist in Promoting Recovery of Traumatized Young Children.* More recently, on March 14, 2003, Dr. Judith Gardner and Dr. Bernard Karmel, from the New York State Institute for Basic Research in Developmental Disabilities, gave a talk on the *Neurofunctional Approaches to Understanding the High-Risk Infant: Birth to 3 Years.*

Finally, the most recent professional presentations have been on early childhood assessment and an instructional approach for children with autism. On February 6, 2004, Dr. Carol Lidz, in private practice in Philadelphia, offered *A Guided Journey Through Early Childhood Assessment.* And, Susan Julie McGill, the Director of Curriculum and Instruction for Herbert G. Birch Services, gave a presentation on *TEACHH: A Classroom Approach for Children with Autism.* Most recently, on December 3, 2004, Dr. Eleanor Grieg Ukoli, from the New York City Department of Education, distributed materials and presented an update on early childhood education initiatives in New York City.

Beyond offering professional presentations on a variety of topics related to early childhood and infant psychology, NYAECIP has been engaged with a number of research projects. More specifically, a research group within NYAECIP collected data on early childhood and infant psychology practice in New York State. One project collected data on the early childhood and infant psychology practices of New York State certified school psychologists and the other looked at similar issues for a sample of New York State licensed psychologists. The surveys were sent to certified school psychologists and licensed psychologists respectively. Each group was queried about their education, background experience, and training. Further, information was gathered regarding professional practice in early childhood and infant psychology; consultation and collaboration data was collected as well as information regarding continuing professional education needs and preferences. A number of doctoral students from the School-Clinical Child Psychology doctoral program at Pace University-New York City participated in these research efforts (e.g., Goliger, 2002; Kumar, 2002; Sweeney, 2002).

The research regarding the practices, background, and continuing education needs of NYS certified school psychologists and licensed psychologists resulted in the publication of two papers, one on the continuing education needs and another on the collaboration and consultation practices of NYS certified school psychologists. These research papers were published in the American Psychological Association's Division 16's (School Psychology) publication, *The School Psychologist* (Mowder, Goliger, Sossin, & Rubinson, 2003; Rubinson, Sweeny, Mowder, & Sossin, 2003). In addition, a number of professional presentations related to these research projects were presented at the annual meetings of the American Psychological Association and the National Association of School Psychologists, primarily by Drs. Mowder, Rubinson, and Sossin. Students assisting in this research included Scott Galligher, Iris Goliger, Todd Karlin, Neena Kumar, Christopher Quirk, and Karen Sweeney.

Most recently, NYAECIP has embarked on a number of additional projects. Currently, NYAECIP has a web-site at www.nyaecip.net and is working on a directory of early childhood and infant psychology practitioners. Further, NYAECIP is publishing this journal, the *Journal of Early Childhood and Infant Psychology (JECIP)*, and looks forward to furthering the development of the early childhood and infant specialty area in psychology. The current president of NYAECIP is Dr. Anastasia Yasik, Pace University-New York City, and she has outlined a number of initiatives, including updating the NYAECIP web-site and proceeding with the development of an Early Childhood and Infant Psychologist Directory for the metropolitan New York area that would assist parents and educators in finding adequate services for young children.

NYAECIP looks forward to continuing to serve psychologists interested in young children and infants, as well as advocating for these youngsters and their families. One means, in particular, moves the scope of NYAECIP beyond the New York area and that is the journal initiative, the *Journal of Early Childhood and Infant Psychology (JECIP)*. By starting this endeavor, NYAECIP is further meeting the established goals of the organization. More specifically, JECIP provides a medium for networking within early childhood and infant psychology and will foster research, writing, and other interactions among those interested in early childhood and infant psychology. Further, JECIP has the potential to help the field establish early childhood and infant psychology as a recognized specialty within our own profession and, most certainly, will act as a voice for early childhood and infant psychology by serving as an information and communication vehicle for those interested in early childhood and infant psychology developments, issues, research, and training.

References

Goliger, I. (2002). The continuing education interests of New York State early childhood school psychologists. (Doctoral Dissertation, Pace University-New York City, 2002), *Dissertation Abstracts International, 63*, 3007.

Kumar, N. (2002). The training and practice of early childhood school psychologists in New York State. (Doctoral Dissertation, Pace University-New York City, 2002), *Dissertation Abstracts International, 63*, 3854.

Mowder, B. A., Goliger, I., Sossin, K. M., & Rubinson, F. D. (2003). Continuing education interests and needs of New York State early childhood school psychologists. *The School Psychologist, 57,* 130-139.

Rubinson, F. D., Sweeny, K., Mowder, B. A., & Sossin, K. M. (2003). Collaborative practices of early childhood school psychologists in New York State. *The School Psychologist, 57*, 73-85.

Sweeney, K. (2002). School psychological training, practice and the use of consultation/collaboration within infant and early childhood psychology. (Doctoral Dissertation, Pace University-New York City, 2002). *Dissertation Abstracts International, 63*, 3499.

Posttraumatic Stress Disorder in Infants, Toddlers, and Young Children: Diagnostic Considerations

Anastasia E. Yasik, Ph.D.
Pace University

Young children are frequently exposed to traumatic events in the United States and elsewhere throughout the world. An appreciation of the prevalence of trauma exposure and the effect it can have on the social, emotional, and behavioral functioning of young children is essential for clinicians. A historical review of trauma reactions in young children is presented to lay the foundation for appreciation of the long-standing clinical interest in this area. A comparison of the diagnostic classification systems, *Diagnostic and Statistical Manual – IV* (posttraumatic stress disorder) and the *Diagnostic Classification: 0-3* (traumatic stress disorder), is conducted with consideration for their appropriateness with infants, toddlers, and young children. Furthermore, the co-occurrence of behavioral problems is considered within a developmental context and within the context of the diagnostic decision making process. Preliminary research questions the utility of the DSM-IV diagnostic criteria for infants, toddlers, and young children. Extending beyond the child to include parental reactions and observations is imperative in gaining a complete picture of the child's functioning and to implement a most effective intervention.

Prevalence of Trauma Exposure

Young children are frequently exposed to traumatic events in the United States and throughout the world. An appreciation of the prevalence of trauma exposure and the indicators of negative reactions to stress is critical for profes-

All correspondence should be addressed to Anastasia E. Yasik, Ph.D., Pace University, Psychology Department, 41 Park Row, New York, NY 10038. Email may be sent to ayasik@pace.edu

sionals working with young children. According to the National Center for Injury Prevention and Control (NCIPC, 2004), 903,000 children in the United States were at risk for or experienced abuse and or neglect in 2001. The Office of the Press Secretary of the United States reported that in 2002 approximately 900,000 children were victims of abuse or neglect. Physical abuse was evident among 19% of victims and 10% were sexually abused. Similarly, the NCIPC (2001) reports that approximately 30% of rapes occur before the age of 12.

With respect to accident related traumas a host of events (e.g., motor vehicle accidents, dog bites, bicycle accidents, fires) have been investigated and suggest high degrees of traumatic exposure in the early years of life. For example, the 2003 motor vehicle accident injury rate for children less than 5 years was 300 per 100,000 and increased to 372 per 100,000 between the ages of 5-9 years (National Highway Traffic Safety Administration, 2004). Nearly 31,000 children between the ages of 5-14 years accounted for pedestrian-related injuries in 2002 (NCIPC, 2004). With regard to non-motor vehicle accidents the 2003 injury rates were 15 per 100,000 and 59 per 100,000 for less than 5 years of age and 5 to 9 years of age, respectively. Bicycling accidents account for approximately 140,000 children under the age of 15 who are treated for traumatic brain injuries. Furthermore, the risk for dog bites is greater among children, with 2.5% of children per year being bitten by a dog (NCIPC, 2001). In addition, 45% of fireworks-related injuries involved children below the age of 14 years with children 5 to 9 years old being at greatest risk. Similarly, children under 4 are at greater risk for fire-related injuries (NCIPC, 2004). Given the degree of exposure to traumatic events, it is important to understand the reactions infants, toddlers, and children may have to such traumatic events.

History of Stress Reactions in Children

The effects of traumatic experiences on young children have long been of interest to clinicians and researchers. As early as 1937, Bender and Blau examined sixteen children at the Children's Ward of the Psychiatric Division of Bellevue Hospital who had had sexual relations with adults. The authors made specific reference to feelings of fear, avoidance, irritability, nightmares, trauma reenactments, and hypervigilance. In some cases, academic impairment was also indicated. Whereas a great majority of literature during World War II recorded the symptoms of adults exposed to war-related stressors (Saigh, 1992), several researchers (e.g., Bodman, 1941; Mercer & Despert, 1943) examined the psychiatric morbidity of children who were exposed to comparable stressors.

In 1941, Frank Bodman, the Deputy Director of the Bristol Child Guidance Clinic, reported on the findings of a survey examining the incidence of "strain" following the British air-raids on 8,000 British school children ranging in age from five to fourteen years. It was observed that 4% presented with psychological (e.g., nightmares, war-related fears, psycho-physiological reactivity, avoidance, aggressive behaviors) or psychosomatic (e.g., headaches, enuresis, encopresis, indigestion) symptoms. Given that this survey was conducted during a time when raids were still occurring, Bodman conducted a follow-up study with 54 children (age range 2 months to 12 years) who had been evacuated from the Children's Hospital in Bristol. According to Bodman (1941), "soldiers were crunching through a litter of broken glass, fallen plaster, and blown-in black-out material, picking children out of cots and beds and, tucking them under their arms, running down the steps and dumping them pell-mell into the lorry" (p. 486). Up to two months later, 61% of these children showed symptoms that were attributed to the raids. Eleven percent evidenced symptoms seven months afterward. Shortly thereafter, Mercer and Despert (1943) examined the effects of war on French children. These children were reported to suffer from increased heart rate, enuresis, nightmares, trauma-related recollections, memory impairment, and academic impairment.

Subsequent to World War II, Carey-Trefzer (1949) followed 1,203 British school children who were exposed to war-related stressors such as air-raids, evacuation, change in family life, loss of schooling, and housing problems. Of these, 212 (17.6% of the sample) presented with "disturbances caused or aggravated by war experiences" (Carey-Trefzer, 1949, p. 556). Symptoms included irritability, concentration impairment, memory impairment, sleep disturbance, and avoidance behaviors. In addition, 30.6% of the affected youth experienced academic difficulties. Carey-Trefzer concluded that these impairments reflect "the degree to which emotional disturbances affect the capacity to learn" (p. 546).

Bloch, Silber, and Perry (1956) explored the emotional reactions to 185 students attending a public school in Vicksburg, Mississippi. On Saturday December 5, 1953, these youth were exposed to extreme stress when a tornado hit their community causing considerable damage. Forty-seven youth (25.4% of the sample) presented with mild to severe symptoms related to the tornado. Symptoms included trauma specific re-enactments (e.g., tornado games), irritability, hypervigilance, avoidance, and enuresis.

Within the context of criminal victimization, Terr (1979, 1983, 1991) interviewed 26 school children (ages 5-14 years) who had been kidnapped in Chowchilla, California. Children reported a variety of symptoms such as fears, play reenactments of the trauma, personality changes, hallucinations, enuresis, and anniversary reactions. Based on her work with traumatized children, Terr proposed four categories of symptoms common to many children exposed to trauma. These categories included: 1) repetitive memories of the traumatic event; 2) repetitive behaviors (e.g., play, traumatic reenactments); 3) trauma-specific fears; and 4) changed attitudes about people, life, and the future. Terr went on to divide childhood traumas into two basic types. Type I trauma involves single incident, acute traumas. Type II traumas were described as involving repeated exposure to traumatic events such as abuse. Terr further indicated that characteristics of both types of childhood trauma could exist side by side. This represents one of the early attempts at classify children's reactions to traumatic events.

Since that time, more formal diagnostic classifications have developed and been implemented in clinical and research settings. The literature on child and adolescent posttraumatic stress disorder has flourished examining children exposed to war-related stressors, criminal victimization (e.g., sexual abuse, sexual assault), accidents, and natural disasters (Saigh, Yasik, Sack, & Koplewicz, 1999). The great majority of these studies have utilized diagnostic criteria established for adults to formulate diagnoses and have not typically included children younger than the ages of 6 or 7. As such, a consideration for the similarities and differences among available diagnostic criteria is undertaken with implications for diagnosing posttraumatic stress in young children (including infants and toddlers).

Current Diagnostic Classifications

With the publication of the *Diagnostic Statistical Manual-III* (APA, 1980) the diagnostic category of posttraumatic stress disorder (PTSD) was introduced into the diagnostic nomenclature. Not until the DSM-III-R (APA, 1987), however, were children considered in the diagnostic classification of PTSD. Currently two diagnostic classification systems utilized in the United States for classifying stress reactions in infants, toddlers, and young children. These classification systems are the DSM–IV (APA, 1994) and the *Diagnostic Classification of Mental Health and Developmental Disorders of Infancy and Early Childhood* (DC 0-3; Zero to Three/National Center for Clinical Infant Programs, 1994).

The DSM-IV describes PTSD as the development of characteristic symptoms following exposure to "an event or events that involve actual or threatened death or serious injury, or a threat to the physical integrity of oneself or others" (APA, 1994, p. 428). In order to diagnosis PTSD via DSM-IV criteria the person must also present with situational reactivity described as "intense fear, helplessness, or horror" to the event. The three symptom areas for PTSD in the DSM-IV include: reexperiencing of the traumatic event, avoidance of and or numbing related to traumatic reminders, and increased arousal. With respect to diagnosing PTSD in children the DSM-IV presents three diagnostic notes for reexperiencing symptoms. Specifically, "In young children, repetitive play may occur in which themes or aspects of the trauma are expressed". Also, "In children, there may be frightening dreams without recognizable content" and "In young children trauma-specific reenactment may occur". Despite the thorough process (i.e., clinical and community based field trials) that went into developing these criteria, it is of critical importance to those working with young children to recognize that the DSM-IV field trials for PTSD did not include youth below the age of 15 years (Kilpatrick et al., 1998). Thus the applicability of these criteria for children younger than the age of 15 has not been firmly established.

In an attempt to develop a diagnostic nomenclature appropriate for very young children, the Diagnostic Classification: 0-3 (DC: 0-3; Zero to Three, 1994) utilized Task Forces comprised of clinicians and researchers who gathered information from infant and child mental health programs throughout the US, Canada, and Europe to establish diagnostic criteria for a variety of disorders evidenced at this early age (e.g., traumatic stress disorder, disorders of affect, anxiety disorders of infancy and early childhood, mood disorders). Initial diagnostic formulations were developed from behavioral case descriptions and recurring patterns of behavioral problems evidenced. Discussion regarding the information gathered ensued with the development of diagnostic categories based on expert consensus.

As noted in the DC: 0-3:

> Because an infant or young child, in comparison with an adult, is capable of only a limited number of behavioral patterns or responses to various stresses or difficulties (e.g., somatic symptoms, irritability, withdrawal, impulsivity, fears, and developmental delays), some overlap is inevitable. The primary diagnosis should reflect the most prominent features of the disorder (p. 16).

In establishing a diagnosis according to the DC: 0-3 a hierarchy of considerations is indicated. Specifically, if the infant or child has experienced a clear stressor a diagnosis of "traumatic stress disorder" should be considered first. Similar to the DSM-IV this diagnosis is considered when "an infant or toddler's direct experience, witnessing, or confrontation with an event or events that involve actual or threatened death or serious injury to the child or others, or a threat to the psychological or physical integrity of the child or others" (DC: 0-3, 1994, p. 19). However, in contrast to the DSM-IV, the requirement of situational reactivity is not included in the DC: 0-3.

Similar to the diagnostic structure of the DSM-IV the DC: 0-3 classification of traumatic stress disorder includes consideration for re-experiencing, numbing, and increased arousal symptoms; however, differences exist with respect to the exact symptom threshold required for diagnosis. While the DSM-IV requires the presence of one re-experiencing, three avoidance and numbing, and two increased arousal symptoms, the DC: 0–3 requires the presence of only one per symptom cluster to diagnosis traumatic stress disorder. Furthermore, symptoms are described in more developmentally appropriate terminology. Reexperiencing symptoms include: post-traumatic play, recurrent recollections of the traumatic event (e.g., statements or questions about the event), repeated nightmares, distress upon exposure to traumatic reminders, and flashbacks or dissociation objectively noted by observers. The second symptom area includes the following aspects of numbing: increased social withdrawal, restricted range of affect, loss of previously acquired developmental skills, and a decrease or constriction of play. Increased arousal is evidenced by night terrors, difficulty going to sleep, difficulty staying asleep, hypervigilance, and startle response.

In contrast to PTSD as described in the DSM-IV, traumatic stress disorder as described in the 0-3 classification includes the additional category of newly developed symptoms that were not evidenced prior to the traumatic event. This symptom area encompasses several types of aggressive, fear/anxiety, and behavioral difficulties. A summary of the symptoms comprising this category includes: aggressive behaviors towards peers, adults, or animals; separation anxiety, fear of toileting alone, fear of dark, or other fears; manipulative behaviors; provocative behaviors that may provoke abuse; sexual and or aggressive behaviors; immediate nonverbal reactions (e.g., somatic symptoms, motor reenactments); and other new symptoms. Table 1 presents a complete description of the DC: 0–3 diagnostic criteria for traumatic stress disorder.

Scheeringa and colleagues (Scheeringa, Peebles, Cook, & Zeanah, 2001; Scheeringa, Zeanah, Drell, & Larrieu, 1995; Scheeringa, Zeanah, Myers, & Putnam, 2003) in a series of experiments have explored the validity of these diagnostic criteria for use with preschool children relative to the utility of DSM-IV diagnostic criteria. Specifically, Scheeringa et al. (2003) examined sixty-two children aged 20 months to six years who had been exposed to MVA's, injuries, abuse, or witnessed traumas and sixty-three healthy, non-traumatized children. Based on the *Posttraumatic Stress Disorder Semi-Structured Interview and Observation Record for Infants and Young Children* (Sheeringa & Zeanah, 1994), none of the traumatized children met the DSM-IV diagnostic criteria for PTSD. However, 68% of traumatized children evidenced at least one reexperiencing symptom and 45% evidenced two or more increased arousal symptoms. In contrast, only 2% evidenced 3 or more DSM-IV avoidance and numbing symptoms.

Further exploration of the number of avoidance and numbing symptoms required for diagnostic purposes was conducted by Scheeringa et al. (2003), who also explored the utility of including loss of developmental skills within that

Table 1: DC: 0 – 3 Diagnostic Criteria for Traumatic Stress Disorder

1. A re-experiencing of the traumatic event(s) as evidenced by at least one of the following:

   a. Post-traumatic play - that is, play that represents a reenactment of some aspect of the trauma, is compulsively driven, fails to relieve anxiety, and is literal and less elaborate and imaginative than usual. This is seen instead of adaptive play reenactment - that is, play that represents some aspect of the trauma but lacks the other characteristics of post-traumatic play.

   b. Recurrent recollections of the traumatic event outside of play - that is, repeated statements of questions about the event that suggest a fascination with the event or preoccupation with some aspect of the event. Distress is not necessarily apparent.

   c. Repeated nightmares, especially if content can be ascertained and has obvious links to trauma.

   d. Distress at exposure to reminders of the trauma.

   e. Episodes with objective features of a flashback or dissociation - that is, reenactment of the event without any sense of where the ideas for the reenactment are coming from, i.e., the behavior is dissociated from the child's intentionality or sense of purpose.

2. A numbing of responsiveness in a child or interference with developmental momentum, appearing after a traumatic event and revealed by at least one of the following:

   a. Increased social withdrawal.

   b. Restricted range of affect.

   c. Temporary loss of previously acquired developmental skills, e.g., toilet training, language, relating to others.

   d. A decrease or constriction in play compared to the child's pattern before the traumatic event.

3. Symptoms of increased arousal that appear after a traumatic event, as revealed by at least one of the following:

   a. Night terrors - that is, symptoms of an arousal disorder in which the child starts from sleep with a panicky scream has agitated motor movements, is unresponsive and inconsolable, and shows signs of autonomic arousal, such as rapid breathing, racing pulse, and sweating. The episodes tend to occur in the first third of the night and last from one to five minutes.

No content can be ascertained at the time or the following day.

b. Difficulty going to sleep, evidenced by strong bedtime protest or trouble falling asleep.

c. Repeated night waking unrelated to nightmares or night terrors.

d. Significant attentional difficulties and decreased concentration.

e. Hypervigilance.

f. Exaggerated startle response.

4. Symptoms, especially fears or aggression, that were not present before the traumatic event, including at least one of the following:

a. Aggression toward peers, adults or animals.

b. Separation anxiety.

c. Fear of toileting alone.

d. Fear of the dark.

e. Other new fears.

f. Pessimism or self-defeating behavior, manipulativeness (designed to gain control), or masochistic provactiveness (behavior that provokes abuse).

g. Sexual or aggressive behaviors inappropriate for a child's age.

h. Other nonverbal reactions experienced at the time of the trauma, including somatic symptoms, motor reenactments, skin stigmata, pain, or posturing.

i. Other new symptoms.

Note: Criteria from Zero to Three/ National Center for Clinical Infant Programs (1994). Diagnostic Classification of Mental Health and Developmental Disorders of Infancy and Early Childhood. Arlington, VA: Author. Reprinted with permission.

symptom domain. Accordingly, 11% of children evidenced two or more avoid-ance and numbing symptoms and 39% evidenced one or more symptoms. With regard to the inclusion of loss of previously acquired developmental skills, 21% of children lost two or more such symptoms and 52% had the loss of one or more developmental skills. Based on this information, it was proposed that there was insufficient evidence for the inclusion of loss of developmental skills as a diag-nostic criterion. Furthermore, a reduction from three to one avoidance and numbing symptom is considered most efficacious.

Along these same lines, the inclusion of new fears in the DC: 0-3 relative to the DSM-IV criteria was not supported by the work of Sheeringa et al. (2003). In total, 79% of traumatized children presented with new symptoms not present before the trauma. This was the most frequent symptom area and was not con-sidered useful in differentiating children with and without PTSD. As such, the inclusion of this in diagnosing traumatic stress disorder is in question.

Following a petroleum gas leak explosion in a nursery school in Japan, Ohmi et al. (2002) explored the utility of the DSM-IV criteria for diagnosing PTSD and alternative criteria (Scheeringa et al., 1995, 2003) in preschool chil-dren (aged 32 to 73 months). Symptom reports were based on maternal report at 10 days, 6 months and 1 year after the accident for all of the 32 children present at the time of the explosion. At the 6 month time point, no child was considered to meet DSM-IV criteria for PTSD. However, 25% of children at 6 months were considered to have PTSD based on the alternative criteria. This data provides further support for the lack of sensitivity of the DSM-IV in diagnosing traumat-ic stress reactions in infants and toddlers. Clinicians need to consider more age-appropriate diagnostic decision making for this age group.

Comorbidity Issues

Complicating the issue of diagnosis in infants and toddlers is the frequency with which hyperactive behaviors are present in this age group. Young children are frequently referred for disorders of impulse control (e.g., attention deficit hyperactivity disorder [ADHD]) that result in overactivity which parents and caregivers find difficult to manage. These most prominent symptoms however may be masking important underlying etiological factors. Furthermore, this inac-curate emphasis on externalizing problems may impede the identification and implementation of an appropriate intervention.

Thomas and Guskin (2001) explored the relationship between the DSM-III-R/IV and the DC:0-3 diagnoses among a sample of 82 children aged 18 to 47 months who had presented to an early childhood psychiatry clinic due to disrup-tive behaviors. According to DSM criteria, 68.3% of the sample was diagnosed with an emotional (e.g., separation anxiety, anxiety disorder not otherwise spec-ified [NOS], mood disorder NOS), or behavioral disorder (i.e., ADHD, oppositional defiant disorder, disruptive behavior disorder NOS). Of the 34.1% of children with a behavioral disorder, 7.1% were diagnosed with traumatic stress disorder via DC: 0-3. Traumatic stress disorder was also diagnosed in 3.7% of children with a DSM diagnosis of emotional disorder and 3.7% of those with a DSM diagnosis of adjustment disorder. All of the 13.4% of children diagnosed with PTSD according to the DSM were also diagnosed with traumatic stress dis-order via DC: 0-3. In total, 23.2% of children were diagnosed with a traumatic stress disorder. Further exploration of symptom presentation, indicated that 52.6% of those with a traumatic stress disorder had CBCL Externalizing scores considered to be in the clinically significant range.

Along these same lines, Scheeringa et al. (2003) reported that 63% of preschoolers with PTSD had separation anxiety disorder, 38% had ADHD, and 75% oppositional defiant disorder based on DSM-IV diagnostic criteria. Similarly, those preschoolers with PTSD had significantly higher CBCL Total, Internalizing, and Externalizing problem behaviors relative to traumatized preschoolers without PTSD and healthy controls. Similarly, Saigh, Yasik, Oberfield, Halamandaris, and McHugh (2002) reported that 60.9% of children and adolescents with PTSD subsequent to a variety of traumatic events (e.g., sex-ual assaults, physical assaults, motor vehicle accidents) had scores that fell within the clinical range on the CBCL Internalizing scale and 43.5% had scores in the clinical range on the Externalizing scale. Children with PTSD may present with a host of behavioral and affective symptoms that may often divert attention from the possible etiological traumatic event.

Risk Factors

Within a diagnostic decision making framework, it is important to consider factors beyond the traumatic event that may increase the risk of a young child developing traumatic stress disorder. Many variables have been explored as risk factors for the development of PTSD in children. Some of these factors include, but are not limited to, age and or developmental status, gender, intensity of the traumatic event, proximity to the event, personality characteristics of the child, and parental psychopathology (Rojas & Papagallo, 2004; Saigh et al., 1999). In the main, much of the research exploring these risk factors has not included infants and toddlers. Given this particularly vulnerable developmental stage, how parents deal with the traumatic event can be a critical factor in how the child responds.

Laor, Wolmer, Mayes, Gershon, Weizman, and Cohen (1997) conducted a longitudinal study of Israeli preschoolers (aged 3 – 5 years) and their mothers exposed to Scud missile attacks during the Gulf War. These families were divided into the following three groups for comparison purposes: families displaced from their homes due to damage sustained during the war, families not displaced as their homes remained intact, and those from an area not directly hit by missiles. Results indicated that 7.8% of preschoolers evidenced sufficient symptoms of PTSD to warrant a diagnosis. Furthermore, displaced children as well as their mothers evidenced significantly more PTSD symptoms than those in the other two groups. For the entire sample, maternal avoidance symptoms were the only significant predictor of children's symptoms at 30 months.

Within the displaced group, the relationship between maternal and child symptoms was further examined by child's age. Among the 3 year olds, maternal intrusive and avoidant symptoms were significantly correlated with the child's posttraumatic symptoms. Maternal intrusive symptoms only significantly correlated with symptoms in 4 year old children. In contrast, among 5 year olds there was a non-significant relationship between maternal and child symptoms. In light of this information, Laor et al. (1997) concluded that older children were less dependent on maternal reactions than younger children.

More recently, Almqvist and Broberg (1999) examined risk and protective factors among 50 Iranian refugee preschoolers (aged 4 – 8 years) twelve months and three and a half years after they entered Sweden. At both times periods, 18% of the preschoolers meet DSM-IV criteria for PTSD (Almqvist & Brandell-Forsberg, 1995, 1997). Similarly, 18% evidenced symptoms of posttraumatic stress at twelve months with a decrease in symptoms over time. Maternal mental health difficulties were found to be a significant predictor of children's mental health problems, which included symptoms of PTSD plus other symptoms of "psychological disturbance" (Almqvist & Broberg, 1999).

Six to seven months following an industrial accident, in which the ground caved in and there was threat of building collapse three groups of children (ages: 4-13) and their parents were assessed by Vila, Witkowski, Tondini, Perez-Diaz, Mouren-Simeoni, and Jouvet (2001). The three groups consisted of those who had been evacuated from their homes ("disaster"), families from non-evacuated regions ("threatened"), and families from an area not in danger of ground collapse ("control"). Children in the disaster group had significantly higher levels of posttraumatic symptoms on the *Impact of Events Scale – Revised* compared to the threatened and the control groups. This difference was especially evident with respect to avoidance symptoms. Parents, both mothers and fathers, from the disaster group reported poorer mental health on the *General Health Questionnaire* compared to parents from the other two comparison groups. Furthermore, there was a significant positive correlation between the mental health ratings of spouses such that as one spouse reported greater psychological distress the other spouse's distress also increased. Parental mental health also correlated with avoidance symptoms in children. Maternal mental health correlated with intrusive symptoms in children.

These studies emphasize the importance of evaluating the reaction of all family members exposed to traumatic events and not simply focusing on the referred child. Parents may serve as a buffer and resource for traumatized infants, toddlers, and children (Rojas & Papagallo, 2004). Given parental psychological difficulties, their availability to their child may be impaired and thus impede the healing process for young children. Of particular interest is that this relationship was evidenced for both mothers and fathers (Vila et al., 2001). Parental participation is key to the treatment of stress reactions in children and factors that might influence such participation (i.e., parental reactions to traumatic events) should be considered.

Conclusions

Based on the literature reviewed it is evident that the applicability of the DSM-IV diagnostic criteria for PTSD is insufficient for use with young children, especially infants and toddlers. Based on much of the work by Scheeringa et al. (1995, 2001, 2003), it appears that the DSM-IV criteria set symptom thresholds and the requirement of situational reactivity that are insensitive to the presentation of traumatic stress reactions in young children. Instead, clinicians would be well served to consider the DC: 0–3 diagnostic criteria for younger children as evidence suggests these criteria have greater sensitivity for infants and toddlers comparable to the DSM-IV system.

In addition, to diagnostic criteria it is important to consider the context of the traumatic experience and the involvement and reactions of parents. Given that parental psychopathology is denoted as a risk factor for posttraumatic reactions in children (Rojas & Papagallo, 2004; Saigh et al., 1999), this is essential to consider as the diagnosis of traumatic stress disorder in very young children is often based on parental report. Furthermore, parents and caregivers may be focused on externalizing behaviors that are disruptive within the home or school environment. These acting out behaviors may reflect a manifestation of underlying traumatic reactions. Clearly, further investigation into the presentation of traumatic reactions in infants and toddlers is necessary.

References

Almqvist, K., & Broberg, A. G. (1999). Mental health and social adjustment in young refugee children 3-1/2 years after their arrival in Sweden. *Journal of the American Academy of Child and Adolescent Psychiatry, 38*, 723 - 730.

Almqvist, K., & Brandell-Forsberg, M. (1995). Iranian refugee children in Sweden: A study of preschool children exposed to organized violence and forced migration. *American Journal of Orthopsychiatry, 65*, 225-237.

Almqvist, K., & Brandell-Forsberg, M. (1997). Refugee children in Sweden: Posttraumatic stress disorder in children exposed to organized violence. *Child Abuse and Neglect, 21*, 351-366.

American Psychiatric Association (1980). *Diagnostic and Statistical Manual of Mental Disorders* (3rd ed.). Washington, DC: Author.

American Psychiatric Association (1987). *Diagnostic and Statistical Manual of Mental Disorders* (3rd ed. - Revised). Washington, DC: Author.

American Psychiatric Association (1994). *Diagnostic and Statistical Manual of Mental Disorders* (4th ed.). Washington, DC: Author.

Bender, L., & Blau, A. (1937). The reaction of children to sexual relations with adults. *American Journal of Orthopsychiatry, 7*, 500-518.

Bloch, D. A., Silber, E., & Perry, S. E. (1956). Some factors in the emotional reactions of children to disaster. *American Journal of Psychiatry, 112*, 416-422.

Bodman, F. (1941). War conditions and the mental health of the child. *British Medical Journal, 11*, 486-488.

Carey-Trefzer, C. J. (1949). The results of a clinical study of war-damaged children who attended a child guidance clinic. *Journal of Mental Science, 95*, 535-559.

Kilpatrick, D. G., Resnick, H. S., Freedy, J. R., Pelcovitz, D., Resick, P., Roth,S., & van der Kolk, B. (1998). Posttraumatic stress disorder field trial: Evaluation of the PTSD construct – Criteria A through E. In T. Widiger, J. Frances, H. A. Pincus, R. Ross, M. First, W. Davis, & M. Kline (Eds.), *DSM-IV Sourcebook* (Vol. 4).Washington, DC: American Psychiatric Publishing, Inc.

Laor, N., Wolmer, L., Mayes, L. C., Gershon, A., Weizman, R., & Cohen, D. J. (1997). Israeli preschool children under scuds: A 30-month followup. *Journal of the American Academy of Child and Adolescent Psychiatry, 36*, 349-356.

Mercer, M. H., & Despert, J. M. (1943). Psychological effects of the war on French children. *Psychosomatic Medicine, 5*, 266-272.

National Highway Traffic Safety Administration (NHTSA). (2004). *Traffic safety facts 2003: A compilation of motor vehicle crash data from the fatality analysis reporting system and the general estimates system.* Washington, D.C.: National Center for Statistics and Analysis. Retrieved December 22, 2004, from http://www-nrd.nhtsa.dot.gov/pdf/nrd30/NCSA/TSFAnn/TSF2003EarlyEdition.pdf

National Center for Injury Prevention and Control. (2001). *Injury fact book 2001-2002.* Atlanta, GA: Centers for Disease Control and Prevention. Retrieved December 22, 2004, from http://www.cdc.gov/ncipc/fact_book/factbook.htm.

National Center for Injury Prevention and Control. (2004). *Injuries among children and adolescents: Fact sheets.* Atlanta, GA: Centers for Disease Control and Prevention. Retrieved December 20, 2004, from http://www.cdc.gov/ncipc/factsheets/children.htm.

Ohmi, H., Kojima, S., Awai, Y., Kamata, S., Sasaki, K., Tanaka, Y., et al. (2002). Post-traumatic stress disorder in pre-school aged children after a gas explosion. *European Journal of Pediatrics, 161*, 643-648.

Rojas, V. M., & Papagallo, M. (2004). Risk factors for PTSD in children and adolescents. In R. R. Silva (Ed.), *Posttraumatic stress disorder in children and adolescents, handbook* (pp. 38-59).New York: Norton Publications.

Saigh, P. A. (1992). History, current nosology, and epidemiology. In P. A. Saigh (Ed.), *Posttraumatic stress disorder: A behavioral approach to assessment and treatment* (pp. 1-27). Boston: Allyn & Bacon.

Saigh, P. A., Yasik, A. E., Oberfield, R. A., Halamandaris, P. V., & McHugh, M. (2002). An analysis of the internalizing and externalizing behaviors of traumatized urban youth with and without PTSD. *Journal of Abnormal Psychology, 3*, 462-470.

Saigh, P. A., Yasik, A. E., Sack, W. H., & Koplewicz, H. S. (1999). Child-adolescent posttraumatic stress disorder: Prevalence, risk factors and comorbidity. In P. A. Saigh & J. D. Bremner (Eds.), *Posttraumatic stress disorder: A comprehensive textbook* (pp. 18-43). Boston: Allyn & Bacon.

Scheeringa, M. S., Peebles, C. D., Cook, C. A., & Zeanah, C. H. (2001). Toward establishing procedural, criterion, and discriminant validity for PTSD in early childhood. *Journal of the American Academy of Child and Adolescent Psychiatry, 40*, 52-60.

Scheeringa, M. S., & Zeanah, C. H. (1994). *Semi-Structured interview and observational record for the diagnosis of PTSD in infants and young children (0-48 months)*. New Orleans: Tulane University School of Medicine.

Scheeringa, M. S., Zeanah, C. H., Drell, M. J., & Larrieu, J. A. (1995). Two approaches to the diagnosis of posttraumatic stress disorder in infancy and early childhood. *Journal of the American Academy of Child and Adolescent Psychiatry, 34*, 191-200.

Scheeringa, M. S., Zeanah, C. H., Myers, L., & Putnam, F. W. (2003). New findings on alternative criteria for PTSD in preschool children. *Journal of the American Academy of Child and Adolescent Psychiatry, 42*, 561-570.

Terr, L. C. (1979). Children of Chowchilla: A study of psychic trauma. *Psychoanalytic Study of the Child, 34*, 547-623.

Terr, L. C. (1983). Chowchilla revisited: The effect of psychic trauma four years after a school-bus kidnapping. *American Journal of Psychiatry, 140*, 1543-1550.

Terr, L. C. (1991). Childhood traumas: An outline and overview. *American Journal of Psychiatry, 148*, 10-20.

Thomas, J. M., & Guskin, K. A. (2001). Disruptive behavior in young children: What does it mean? *Journal of the American Academy of Child and Adolescent Psychiatry, 40*, 44-51.

Vila, G., Witkowski, P., Tondini, M. C., Perez-Diaz, F., Mouren-Simeoni, M. C., & Jouvent, R. (2001). A study of posttraumatic disorders in children who experienced an industrial disaster in the Briey region. *European Child and Adolescent Psychiatry, 10*, 10-18.

Zero to Three/ National Center for Clinical Infant Programs (1994). *Diagnostic Classification of Mental Health and Developmental Disorders of Infancy and Early Childhood*. Arlington, VA: Author.

The ACT Training Program:
The Future of Violence Prevention
Aimed at Young Children and Their Caregivers

Michelle Guttman and Barbara A. Mowder
Pace University-New York City

The presence of violence in a young child's life can be seen by watching the news, reading the newspaper, or observing children in school. Exposure to or witnessing violence in the family, media and/or community can have detrimental effects on children's development, especially for very young children. What children observe during this early period of life shapes how they react in other situations or conflicts that might arise. Further, when children observe violence, the likelihood of responding in aggressive ways and developing further problems as they mature increases. Presently, the majority of violence prevention programs tend to work directly with children and do not have a training component for adults who are pivotal in young children's development. Therefore, there are needs for effective violence prevention programs that focus on the role models in young children's lives, such as their parents, caregivers, teachers and others who directly interact with them. One such program is the Adults and Children Together (ACT) Against Violence Training Program. The ACT Training Program provides the adults in children's lives with information on the importance of early prevention, the negative effects violence has on children, and strategies to promote positive outcomes. Therefore, this program may lay the foundation for the development of future violence prevention programs aimed at young children.

There are a number of early violence prevention programs that have been evaluated with regard to their success at reducing the effects of violence on young children. These programs include Childreach (Goodwin, Pacey, & Grace, 2003), Second Step: A Violence Prevention Curriculum (Grossman et al., 1997), Resolving Conflict Creatively Program (Aber, Jones, Brown, Chaudry, & Samples, 1998), PeaceBuilders (Flannery et al., 2003), The Incredible Years (Taylor, Schmidt, Pepler, & Hodgins, 1998), and The RETHINK Parenting and Anger Management Program (Fetsch, Schultz, & Wahler, 1999).

Childreach was created in 1995 at the request of the early childhood education community in Cincinnati. More specifically, there were concerns related to the number of children in early childhood centers exhibiting severe, aggressive behavior (Goodwin et al., 2003). Childreach is an early identification, short-term intervention program for children under the age of 6 and was designed to address aggression as well as other behavioral issues. This program begins with a referral from a child care center director, parent or caregiver and moves through a series of steps designed to shape services around the child's needs. These steps include consultation with staff and parents, observation, intervention for the child and family (e.g., social skills training, developmental intervention, classroom management strategies, and parent training), staff training, referral liaison services, and ongoing support of the child care setting and parents. Since the program's beginning, Childreach has served more than 500 children. To assess whether improvements in behavior were evident after this intervention, Goodwin et al. (2003) used a pre/post method of assessment with a teacher-rated measure of adjustment, the Child and Adolescent Adjustment Profile. Specifically, the evaluations of the children revealed significant improvements in all areas of behavior (e.g., hostility, peer relations, withdrawal, and productivity) except in the area of dependency. In addition, preschool teachers and child care staff reported high levels of satisfaction with the Childreach program. Overall, the data demonstrate that Childreach is an effective secondary prevention program for decreasing violent and aggressive behavior in preschoolers.

Another violence prevention program is Second Step: A Violence Prevention Curriculum (Grossman et al., 1997). Second Step is a social and emotional skills curriculum that aims to teach children to change attitudes and behaviors that contribute to violence. This is accomplished by having teachers focus on developing children's emotional understanding, empathy, impulse control, problem solving and anger management skills through 30 specific lessons (Grossman et al., 1997). In addition to the teacher training, there is a companion program that teaches parents to practice and reinforce prosocial behaviors at home. Grossman et al. evaluated whether Second Step results in a reduction in aggressive behavior and an increase in prosocial behavior among elementary school children. This study utilized a randomized treatment control design and the participants included 790 second and third grade students. Results show that physical aggression decreases and prosocial behavior increases among students who are in the Second Step program.

Resolving Conflict Creatively Program (RCCP) is a prevention program that teaches students that they have many choices for dealing with conflict besides passivity or aggression (Aber et al., 1998). This program also focuses on helping students develop the skills needed to make those choices. This program is for teachers, parents, school administrators and others working with children in grades K-12. The components of the RCCP involve teacher training and coaching, classroom instruction by the trained teachers, administrator training, parent training and peer mediation (i.e., to train selected students to serve their school as peer mediators). The training, consisting of an average of 25 sessions during the school year, seeks to change the classroom, peer group and school contexts in which children learn how to resolve conflict. Aber et al. (1998) evaluated the impact of RCCP on 5,053 children from grades two to six. Results from this study reveal a significant positive impact on children who receive a substantial amount of instruction in the RCCP curriculum, as opposed to those who have less instruction in RCCP. This includes increases in prosocial behavior, problem solving and academic success, and decreases in aggressive and destructive behaviors (Aber et al., 1998).

PeaceBuilders is a universal (i.e., school wide), elementary school based violence prevention program that aims to change the school climate by teaching students, staff and parents rules and activities to improve social competence and reduce aggressive behavior in children (Flannery et al., 2003). In PeaceBuilders, the program is purposely woven into the school's everyday routine rather than in a time or subject limited process. In a study conducted by Flannery et al. (2003), more than 4000 students from eight matched schools were randomly assigned to either the immediate post-baseline intervention group or to a delayed intervention group. In this study, the delayed intervention group received the PeaceBuilders program one year after the immediate intervention group, who continued to receive the program in the second year. Flannery et al. finds that participation in the PeaceBuilders program improves students' social competence. In addition, declines in teacher-reported aggressive behavior were found, especially for children in the program for two years. These results highlight the importance of intervening early in children's lives to help put them on a positive developmental course that can be maintained over time. Beyond asserting the importance of intervention, Flannery et al. also stresses the importance of early preventive interventions, especially strategies focusing on increasing positive skills as well as those targeting a reduction in aggressive behaviors of young children.

The Incredible Years is a research-based curriculum for reducing children's aggression and behavior problems and increasing their social and emotional competence at home and at school (Taylor et al., 1998). There are separate programs for parents, teachers, childcare providers and children ages three to eight. In the parent training component, there is an emphasis on nonviolent discipline strategies and teaching children problem solving skills, anger management and social skills. With teachers, there is training on the importance of praise, help in decreasing inappropriate behavior in the classroom, and strategies to promote children's social and emotional competence in school. For children, there is empathy training, learning rules, problem solving, anger management, how to make friends and how to be successful in school. In six randomized studies by Taylor et al. (1998), home, laboratory and classroom observations show that The Incredible Years' parent, teacher and child programs are effective in reducing aggressive behaviors in children; these results are sustained in two and three year follow-up studies.

Last, the RETHINK Parenting and Anger Management Program is a research-based, preventive educational workshop for parents, educators, and other professionals working with young children (Fetsch et al., 1999). The RETHINK Program provides materials for teaching parents how to manage their anger and how to teach anger management skills to their children. Fetsch et al. (1999) evaluated the RETHINK program with 75 parents using a one-group, pretest-posttest design. Participants received a six-week series of skill-enhancing workshops (a full day workshop for parent educators, a six-week program for parents). This preliminary evaluation indicates that the RETHINK Parenting and Anger Management Program reduces family conflict, domestic physical and verbal aggression as well as results in positive changes in parenting and anger management skills (Fetsch et al., 1999). In addition, all of the participants report that their knowledge about parenting and anger management increased as a direct result of participating in RETHINK. These results suggest that the RETHINK Program is an effective program for assisting parents with anger management. Despite the promising results, Fetsch et al. report that one limitation of their study is their failure to obtain a no-treatment comparison group.

The results of these evaluation studies (i.e., Aber et al., 1998; Fetsch et al., 1999; Flannery et al., 2003; Goodwin et al., 2003; Grossman et al., 1997; Taylor et al., 1998) provide evidence for the effectiveness of early intervention programs in breaking the potentially dangerous chain of events leading to violence and aggression in children. Thus, early prevention and intervention efforts can lessen aggression in elementary school aged children (Leff, Power, Manz, Costigan, & Nabors, 2001). One such program that has yet to be evaluated is the Adults and Children Together (ACT) Against Violence Prevention Program, which is the focus of this paper.

The Adults and Children Together (ACT) Against Violence Prevention Program

Overview

The Adults and Children Together (ACT) Against Violence Prevention Program began in December 2000. This program was developed by the American Psychological Association (APA) and the National Association for the Education of Young Children (NAEYC) along with the assistance from experts on child development and violence prevention (DaSilva, Sterne, & Anderson, 2000). The ACT Training Program is based on research demonstrating that the early years (i.e., ages 0-8) constitute a critical time when children are learning basic skills that have a long-lasting impact on their lives. Due to this tenet, the theme of the ACT Training Program is, "What a child learns about violence, a child learns for life." The goal of ACT is to disseminate research-based knowledge on young children and violence prevention to those who work with young children to help children be nonaggressive in their way of solving problems they encounter (DaSilva et al., 2000).

The ACT Training Program was developed to do the following: offer early violence prevention knowledge and skills to professionals and other adults in young children's lives; provide a program built on knowledge gained from research-based violence prevention information focusing on young children; and to encourage collaboration among community organizations to address early violence prevention (DaSilva et al., 2000). Unlike many other violence prevention programs, ACT focuses solely on adults and is designed to help adults learn how to teach and model positive ways for young children to deal with anger and resolve conflicts.

The ACT Training Program is a social-cognitive intervention because the program is based on the assumptions that children learn by observing and imitating adults and others, violence results in part from an individual's lack of problem-solving and social skills needed to deal with conflicts, and that adults can learn to model and teach skills that will help children deal with their social relationships in a nonaggressive way (DaSilva et al., 2000). The ACT Training Program consists of four modules on important skills for early violence prevention: Anger Management, Social Problem Solving, Discipline and Media Violence. Each of these modules is described below.

Anger Management

Children who have high levels of anger and do not possess the skills necessary to regulate these negative emotions are prone to behavioral problems and peer difficulties. When concentrating on younger children, such as preschoolers, emotional competence is defined as the child's ability to understand others' emotions, to react to others' emotions and to regulate their own emotional expressiveness (Denham, Blair, Schmidt, & DeMulder, 2002; Halberstadt, Denham, & Dunsmore, 2001). Denham et al. (2002) notes that young children who are frequently angry are unable to react calmly in difficult situations, may misconstrue others' emotional signals, and are unable to interact successfully with their peers. As a result of their underregulated anger and misperceiving others' emotions, these children are likely to evidence emotional competence deficits and externalizing difficulties.

In a longitudinal study conducted by Denham et al. (2002), data was collected on 91 children at the age of three or four years old and again when they were in kindergarten. The purpose of this study was to see if emotional incompetence led to evaluations of social incompetence two years later. To obtain their data, Denham et al. observed and interviewed children in preschool, and later in kindergarten, and administered questionnaires (e.g., The Social Competence and Behavior Evaluation-Short Form) to the children's teachers. Results find that preschool children, who show a great deal of unregulated anger, have problems with oppositionality two years later in kindergarten. The results of this study show that regulation of emotion is an important ability for managing the demands inherent in interpersonal situations. Due to these findings, Denham et al. stress the need for early childhood prevention and intervention programs that focus on anger management and social problem solving. Focusing on these two issues is one way to curtail the difficulties that are likely to persist if not addressed early in children's lives.

Young children who are angry are unable to react calmly in different situations. These children may misconstrue others' emotional signals, which affect their ability to interact in a satisfying way with peers (Denham et al., 2002). Therefore, to help children express their anger, The ACT Training Program dedicates one of their four modules to anger management. The objective of the Anger Management module is for those working with young children to learn skills to help children express anger appropriately and to channel their angry feelings into constructive actions (DaSilva et al., 2000). To accomplish this, the Anger Management module focuses on such topics as helping children manage anger effectively, helping adults express and channel their anger, anger management as a violence prevention asset, child development issues and developing anger management skills.

Social Problem Solving

Mayeux and Cillessen (2003) highlight the fact that two decades of empirical research has shown that children's success or failure in being accepted by peers is determined in part by their skill in social problem solving. Mayeux and Cillessen studied 231 kindergarten and first grade boys who were classified by their peers as liked or disliked (i.e., accepted or rejected) in order to examine their social problem solving strategies when given hypothetical social dilemmas. Results indicate that popular boys are more likely to request that a solution be reached, to be assertive and to respond prosocially than the less popular peers, who use the ineffective strategies of avoidance and manipulation. Therefore, given the link between social competence and peer acceptance, it is likely that children's use of social problem solving strategies become stable in later childhood and this could have a negative impact on the children who are rejected by peers (Mayeux & Cillessen). Due to this process, the authors stress the need for the development of early intervention programs to improve a wide range of children's social behaviors. Mayeux and Cillessen suggest that rejected children be taught to use effective means of conflict resolution, such as responding prosocially, through early intervention programs that focus on improving a wide range of social behavior (e.g., emotional regulation, social cognition, behavioral responses).

In another study, Schwartz and Proctor (2000) examined the relationship between community violence exposure and peer group social maladjustment. Schwartz and Proctor note that violence exposure has a detrimental effect on children's peer relationships and might lead to the development of social-cognitive biases or deficits that are associated with problematic social behaviors such as aggression. In this study, 285 inner-city fourth and fifth graders (mean age = 10 years) from two schools participated. The children completed an inventory assessing exposure to community violence and a peer nomination inventory to assess social adjustment with peers. The findings indicate that there is a moderately strong link between community violence exposure and negative social outcomes in the peer group (Schwartz & Proctor). Community violence exposure appears to be associated with many areas of risk, predicting emotional and behavioral difficulties as well as problematic social functioning with peers. These findings suggest the importance of the early development of problem solving abilities for social competence with peers and when dealing with conflict.

Based on research showing the importance of social skills in children's lives (i.e., Mayeux & Cillessen, 2003; Schwartz & Proctor, 2000), the ACT Training Program includes social problem solving as one of their modules. This module's objective is for early childhood professionals to be able to identify strategies they can use to teach social problem solving skills to young children and to be able to help families of young children teach these skills in the home environment (DaSilva et al., 2000). The Social Problem Solving module covers topics such as the importance of teaching social problem skills, a developmental view of when children can learn social skills, the role of families and others working with young children in teaching these skills and social problem solving activities.

Discipline

Harsh discipline strategies have been shown to have negative effects on children's development. For example, Weiss, Dodge, Bates and Pettit (1992) examined whether harsh physical discipline was predictive of aggressive and/or internalizing behavior in children. They also examined the impact of physical discipline on children's social information processing patterns. In the sample, two cohorts of children were selected at kindergarten entrance. The first cohort sample had 309 children and the second contained 275 children. The parents filled out a number of questionnaires and were interviewed by a trained individual. The children's social information processing patterns were assessed through a series of vignettes depicting hostile, benign or ambiguous social situations in which the children had to process and respond to the social event. Teacher measures assessing aggression and behavioral observations were also employed. Results indicate that for each cohort, early physical punishment was positively correlated with children's aggressive behavior in the child as measured by parent and teacher ratings as well as direct observation (Weiss et al., 1992). In addition, higher levels of harsh discipline are associated with greater processing biases and difficulties in both cohorts. Therefore, the consequences of early harsh discipline may be that the child becomes aggressive and develops a maladaptive style of processing social information, which might be related to the development of aggression (Weiss et al.).

Physical discipline is not the only type of discipline that has detrimental effects on children. Straus and Field (2003) investigated the prevalence of psychological aggression in a nationally representative sample of 991 parents (i.e., data collected from a national telephone survey conducted by the Gallup Organization). In this research, Straus and Field defined psychological aggression as "a communication intended to cause the child to experience psychological pain; the communicative act may be active or passive or verbal or nonverbal" (p. 797). Results indicate that by the age of two years, 90% of parents report using one or more forms of psychological aggression during the previous 12 months and 98% report this use by the age of five. From the ages of six to 17, the rates of psychological aggression continue in the 90% range. The rate of severe psychological aggression is lower, with 1%-20% for toddlers and 50% for teenagers (Straus & Field). This study shows that even infants are not exempt from being yelled at when parents are angry. For the long-term effects, psychological aggression is shown to be associated with higher rates of delinquency and psychological problems. Straus and Field emphasize that avoiding discipline techniques that involve psychological and physical aggression increases the probability of children being well adjusted.

Due to the research showing the harmful effects of harsh discipline on children, the ACT Training Program includes discipline as a module. The objective of the Discipline module is to teach strategies for responding to young children's challenging behavior and to help adults in children's lives to create a plan to use for preventing and managing those behaviors (DaSilva et al., 2000). A number of topics are discussed in the Discipline module, including the relationship between discipline and violence prevention, child development issues, the distinction between discipline and punishment, and strategies for responding to challenging behavior.

Media Violence

The body of literature on children's exposure to media violence (i.e., television shows, movies, video games and music) supports the idea that viewing violence is a contributing factor to the development of aggression. Huesmann, Moise-Titus, Podolski, and Eron (2003) conducted a follow-up study of their 1977 longitudinal study of 557 children looking at whether children's television habits predict subsequent aggression. The aim of their study was to investigate the long-term relations between viewing media violence in childhood and young adult aggressive behavior. Of the original 557, Huesmann et al. (2003) were able to locate 329 of the original sample. Results indicate that children's television viewing between ages six and nine, their identification with aggressive same-sex television characters, and their perceptions that television violence is realistic are significantly correlated with adult aggression for both males and females. The stronger amount/belief of each of those variables predicted more adult aggression regardless of how aggressive the individuals were as children. Overall, males and females are at an increased risk for the development of aggressive and violent behavior when they are exposed to high amounts of media violence in early childhood.

In another study, Anderson et al. (2003) looked at the research pertaining to violent television and films, video games and music and found consistent evidence that media violence increases the likelihood of aggressive and violent behavior in both immediate and long-term contexts. Specifically, short-term exposure increases the likelihood of physically and verbally aggressive behavior, aggressive thoughts and aggressive emotions. Media violence produces long-term effects consisting of the acquisition of lasting aggressive scripts and aggression supporting beliefs about social behavior. Anderson et al. indicate that even brief exposure to violent scenes on television causes short-term increases in children's aggressive thoughts, emotions and behaviors.

With regards to violent video games, the studies reviewed all provide support for a connection between playing violent games and the increased likelihood of engaging in aggression (Anderson et al., 2003). Since children are active participants in these games and not just observers, like they are when watching television, the active participation may place them at an increased risk for becoming aggressive. A number of experimental studies demonstrate that in the short term, violent video games cause increases in aggressive thoughts, actions and behavior, increases in physiological arousal and decreases in helpful behavior (Anderson et al.). Due to the findings of Anderson et al., the need for educating parents and professionals on the effects of media violence on children and their development is clear.

Based on the wealth of research demonstrating the negative effects of media violence on young children (e.g., Anderson et al., 2003; Huesmann & Miller, 1994; Huesmann et al., 2003; Wood, Wong, & Chachere, 1991) the ACT Training Program includes this topic as one of their four modules. In the Media Violence module, the objective is to teach the adults in young children's lives about the relationship between exposure to media violence and aggressive behavior (DaSilva et al., 2000). The topics covered in this module include the impact of media violence on young children's lives, child development issues on how children view television differently by age, and strategies to reduce the impact of media violence on young children.

Implications for Violence Prevention

Clearly there are impressive efforts regarding violence prevention aimed at young children and their guardians and caregivers. One of these programs, the ACT Against Violence Program, is comprehensive in nature, focusing on adults in young children's lives. Although the ACT Program is based on research literature regarding violence and violence prevention, research efforts are needed to evaluate the effectiveness of this program. Evaluation research would not only identify potential success efforts, but, in addition, point out avenues for revision and modification. Regardless of the lack of extensive research regarding ACT and the other violence prevention programs, efforts in these directions are important since violence is rife in our society and efforts to promote violence prevention are crucial for the health and well-being of children as well as our society as a whole (Berman, Kurtines, Silverman, & Serafini, 1996).

References

Aber, J. L., Jones, S. M., Brown, J. L., Chaudry, N., & Samples, F. (1998). Resolving conflict creatively: Evaluating the developmental effects of a school-based violence prevention program in neighborhood and class-room context. *Development and Psychopathology, 10*, 187-213.

Anderson, C. A., Berkowitz, L., Donnerstein, E., Huesmann, L. R., Johnson, J. D., Linz, D., et al. (2003). The influence of media violence on youth. *Psychological Science In The Public Interest, 4*(3), 81-110.

Berman, S., Kurtines, W., Silverman, W., & Serafini, L. (1996). The impact of exposure to crime and violence on urban youth. *American Journal of Orthopsychiatry, 66*(3), 329-335.

DaSilva, J., Sterne, M. L., & Anderson, M. P. (2000). *ACT Against Violence training program manual.* Washington, DC: American Psychological Association and National Association for the Education of Young Children.

Denham, S. A., Blair, K., Schmidt, M., & DeMulder, E. (2002). Compromised emotional competence: Seeds of violence sown early? *American Journal of Orthopsychiatry, 72*(1), 70-82.

Fetsch, R., Schultz, C., & Wahler, J. (1999). A preliminary evaluation of the Colorado RETHINK Parenting and Anger Management Program. *Child Abuse and Neglect, 23*(4), 353-360.

Flannery, D. J., Vazsonyi, A. T., Liau, A. K., Guo, S., Powell, K. E., Atha, H., et al. (2003). Initial behavior outcomes for the PeaceBuilders universal school-based violence prevention program. *Developmental Psychology, 39*(2), 292-308.

Goodwin, T., Pacey, K., & Grace, M. (2003). Childreach: Violence prevention in preschool settings. *Journal of Child and Adolescent Psychiatric Nursing, 16*(2), 52-60.

Grossman, D. C., Neckerman, H. J., Koepsell, T. D., Liu, P., Asher, K. N., Beland, K., et al. (1997). Effectiveness of a violence prevention cur-riculum among children in elementary school. *Journal of the American Medical Association, 277*(20), 1605-1611.

Halberstadt, A., Denham, S. A., & Dunsmore, J. (2001). Affective social com-petence. *Social Development, 10*, 79-119.

Huesmann, L. R., & Miller, L. S. (1994). Long-term effects of repeated exposure to media violence in childhood. In L. R. Huesmann (Eds.), *Aggressive Behavior: Current Perspectives* (pp. 153-186). New York: Plenum Press.

Huesmann, L. R., Moise-Titus, J., Podolski, C., & Eron, L. D.   (2003). Longitudinal relations between children's exposure to TV violence and their aggressive and violence behavior in young adulthood: 1977-1992. *Developmental Psychology, 39*(2), 201-221.

Leff, S. S., Power, T. J., Manz, P. H., Costigan, T. E., & Nabors, L. A. (2001). School-based aggression prevention programs for young children: Current status and implications for violence prevention. *School Psychology Review, 30*(3), 344-362.

Mayeux, L., & Cillessen, A. H. (2003). Development of social problem solving in early childhood: Stability, change and associations with social competence. *The Journal of Genetic Psychology, 164*(2), 153-173.

Schwartz, D., & Proctor, L. J. (2000). Community violence exposure and children's social adjustment in the school peer group: The mediating roles of emotion regulation and social cognition. *Journal of Consulting and Clinical Psychology, 68*(4), 670-683.

Straus, M. A., & Field, C. J. (2003). Psychological aggression by American parents: National data on prevalence, chronicity and severity. *Journal of Marriage and Family, 65*, 795-808.

Taylor, T. K., Schmidt, F., Pepler, D., & Hodgins, H. (1998). A comparison of eclectic treatment with Webster-Stratton's Parents and Children Series in a Children's Mental Health Center: A randomized controlled trial. *Behavior Therapy, 29*, 221-240.

Weiss, B., Dodge, K. A., Bates, J. E., & Pettit, G. S. (1992). Some consequences of early harsh discipline: Child aggression and a maladaptive social information processing style. *Child Development, 63*, 1321-1335.

Wood, W., Wong, F. Y., & Chachere, J. G. (1991). Effects of media violence on viewers' aggression in unconstrained social interaction. *Psychological Bulletin, 109*(3), 371-383.

Giving Psychology Away: Educating Adults to ACT Against Early Childhood Violence

Julia M. Silva & Adrienne Randall
American Psychological Association

After decades of involvement (in the forefront of behavioral research, publications, and professional meetings) addressing aggression and violence, the American Psychological Association Public Interest Directorate wanted to "give psychology away" and disseminate to a larger public the findings about child development, media impact on children, violence against children, and violence prevention. Despite the knowledge about the importance of early interventions to prevent the development of violent behaviors, programs that focus on young children are critically lacking. The *ACT—Adults and Children Together— Against Violence* program (ACT) was created to fill this gap by translating research findings on early childhood development, violence and aggression, and prevention science into a comprehensive intervention.

ACT Against Violence is a national anti-violence initiative developed by the American Psychological Association (APA) in collaboration with the National Association for the Education of Young Children (NAEYC), emphasizing the importance of early prevention and the role of adults in providing a learning environment for young children that helps to protect them from violence and injury. The ACT Program builds on research from the social learning theory, based on the principle that "people are not born with preformed repertoires of aggressive behavior. They must learn them" (Bandura, 1973). The major premise of the program is that children learn through observation of others and from experience, and behavior is often modeled after prior experiences of the individual. Research has also indicated that children who witness or experience violence or abuse in their home and community are more likely to grow up and become aggressive and violent (Eron, Gentry, & Schlegel, 1994). Children who do not learn alternatives to violent behaviors may also grow up to become violent.

Based on the categories outlined in the Centers for Disease Control and Prevention (CDC) publication *Best Practices of Youth Violence Prevention* (Thornton, Craft, Dahlberg, Lynch, & Baer, 2002), the ACT Training Program can be defined as a social-cognitive intervention that is based on the following assumptions:

- Violence results in part from an individual's lack of the problem-solving and social skills needed to deal with conflicts;
- Children learn by observing and imitating adults and others;
- If children learn social skills, they can improve their ability to avoid becoming involved in aggressive and violent situations; and,
- Adults can learn to model and teach social skills that will help children deal with their social relationships in a non-aggressive way.

There is evidence that effective parenting is a powerful tool for reducing youth problems; and the critical role of families has been acknowledged by theories of child development (Kumpfer & Alvarado, 2003). Families can be a powerful protective factor when using positive discipline, monitoring and supervising children's actions, having a healthy relationship with their children and modeling positive social skills. In focusing on the early years, the ACT program underscores two critical strategies: the importance of having early intervention/primary prevention as part of interventions, and strengthening parenting skills as a way to influence children's behaviors and prevent violence.

As a result of this body of research, ACT is designed to address violence prevention in early childhood through a unique approach: focus on the adults who are the most influential people in young children's lives: parents, other family members, teachers, and other caregivers, to underscore their important role in preventing youngsters' involvement in violence.

The ACT Program has two components: a national multimedia public service advertising campaign and training programs. *The ACT National Media Campaign* goal is to increase adults' awareness of their important role in shaping children's lives and environments. The campaign was developed under the sponsorship of The Advertising Council and was launched in April 2001 with public service announcements (PSAs) for TV and radio; a website, www.acta-gainstviolence.org; a toll-free number, 1-877-ACT-WISE to call and receive the brochure "Violence Prevention for Families of Young Children"; print ads for newspapers and magazines; and billboards. The third wave of radio and print ads and billboards is currently under production and will be released by the Ad Council in March 2005.

The ACT National Training Program

Introduction

The *ACT National Training Program* goals are: 1) make early violence prevention part of the communities' efforts to prevent violence and 2) educate adults to be positive role models for children. The program and its materials were

developed by APA and NAEYC with assistance from experts in child development, early childhood education, violence prevention, and community
interventions.

The training program is delivered through a 3-day annual national workshop
organized by APA and held in Washington, DC and at local communities by
ACT-trained professionals; it is designed as a train-the-trainer model to prepare
groups of professionals and community members from all over the country to
create opportunities to disseminate research-based information and skills regarding early violence prevention to adults in their communities. Professionals are
prepared to work in collaboration with others in their communities and organize
workshops, trainings, presentations, and special events to disseminate early violence prevention knowledge and skills to adults. The training program began in
2000 and since then, has trained thousands of professionals all over the country.

The training program content addresses 3 major topics: basic elements of
child development, roots and consequences of violence in children's lives, and
early violence prevention skills. A major focal point is the concentration on four
early violence prevention strategies organized in *modules* that can be disseminated to adults: *anger management, social problem solving, positive discipline,
and media literacy.* These four modules build on what is known about child
development, including brain development and the development of cognitive and
emotional processes, the role of a range of risk factors in the development of patterns of aggressive or violent behavior, and the effectiveness of early preventive
interventions. Each module has detailed explanation, activities, and handouts.
All four modules are customized for the intended audience and are presented in
sets for families and teachers of young children.

The *Anger Management* module focuses on helping adults and young children express and manage anger, including expressing feelings appropriately and
how to develop anger management skills. The *Social Problem Solving* module
highlights the importance of learning social problem solving to be applied to
conflict situations. This module also details the role of families in teaching
social problem solving and offers activities for families and teachers to achieve
this objective. The *Discipline* module describes the relationship of discipline to
violence prevention and includes a review of developmentally appropriate disciplinary strategies to prevent challenging behaviors and to plan the adults'
responses. The *Media Violence* module seeks to educate adults to understand
and reduce the impact of media violence on young children; it presents some
strategies to reduce the media impact.

What has been accomplished to date?

Thanks to generous support from the American Psychological Association, MetLife Foundation, David and Lucile Packard Foundation, CDC Foundation, Robert Wood Johnson Foundation, Kellogg Foundation, Foundation for Child Development, and others, much has been accomplished since the ACT program started in 2000. Some highlights include:

- The ACT TV PSA reached more than 60 million American households;
- The radio PSA had more than 150,000 airings;
- 7,000 billboards and 2,500 transit ads have been distributed nationwide, and MetLife Foundation logo was on most of them;
- In total, TV and radio PSAs, outdoor advertisements, print and web-based banner ads have earned more than $ 60 million in donated time and space;
- One hundred and one (101) professionals have been trained at the four annual national workshops conducted so far, 37 of them are psychologists. They have trained more than 1,000 professionals who in turn have reached more than 20,000 adults in the communities;
- There are ACT Training Program sites in communities in 29 states; APA staff provides technical assistance to them on a regular base;
- Thousands of adults have received the program brochures in English and Spanish, flyers, CDs, and videos, through the 800 number, the web site, at the workshops and presentations, and upon request;
- The training program is being implemented in some military bases in the Norfolk, VA area including Fort Eustis, Langley Air Force, Ft Monroe; as well as in the Washington, DC area including Andrews Air Force, Quantico, Walter Reed, Bethesda Naval, and Fort Detrick; there is a potential to expand to other bases across the country.

Evaluation of the ACT Training Program

With support from a contract with the Center for Disease Control's Division of Violence Prevention, the Battelle Centers for Public Health Research and Evaluation conducted the evaluation of the ACT Training Program to assess whether the program is being successfully disseminated and implemented and to examine factors that affect its successful dissemination, adoption, and implementation.

The evaluation design phase involved development of a program logic model and assessment of the information needs of stakeholders, including CDC, ACT program developers, and local ACT implementers and evaluators. Methods of data collection included: collection of archival data, collection of workshop registration data, interviews with program national developers, telephone surveys and focus groups with ACT professionals trained at the 2002 national workshop and with those trained at two workshops conducted in Kansas City area, and telephone surveys with adults in the communities who had been reached by the ACT-trained professionals.

Data was collected and analyzed in 2003 and the major findings in the recently released final report show the majority of those trained by the ACT Program implemented ACT-related activities either in the workplace or the community, with 91.7% of those trained by the national program and 85.3% by the local program in Kansas City. ACT depends on a "ripple effect" to move messages, materials, and activities outward beyond the original source, and data suggest this aspect of the program is working as anticipated. Qualitative data from the facilitator focus groups provide numerous examples of heightened awareness among facilitators about early violence prevention issues. More adults are aware of and can understand early violence prevention. Findings also show there are some longer-term effects in terms of positive changes in adults' attitude and behavior toward children.

Stakeholders at all levels confirmed the quality and attractiveness of ACT materials and the training format. Respondents valued the fact that ACT is grounded in solid research and supported by well-respected national organizations (APA and NAEYC). With its emphasis on early violence prevention and on productive ways for professionals to intervene with parents and caregivers, ACT was viewed as filling an important programmatic gap. The fact that key features of the program were widely observed among respondents suggests that participants emerge from training with an accurate and mutually understood sense of most of the program's core components.

Recommendations from the evaluation study include stabilizing the ACT Program and refraining from making major alterations to the format and materials, increase the involvement of local association affiliates. The strong results from the evaluation study show that the ACT program is meeting its goals and is a successful way to reach out and teach adults knowledge and skills on early violence prevention.

How Can Psychologists Be Involved with the ACT Against Violence Training Program?

Psychologists have been vital for the development and implementation of the ACT Training Program. Some have assisted APA and NAEYC in the development and conceptual design of the program and its materials; have reviewed publications; have provided guidance for programming strategic decisions; have helped in the preparation of grant proposals. Thirty-seven psychologists have been trained by the national program to take ACT to their communities and most of them are actively doing so. Two ACT-trained psychologists are currently involved in studies to assess the impact of the training program on the adults exposed to its research-based content: Dr. Barbara Mowder at Pace University, NY is advising two graduate students who are conducting an evaluation study; and Dr. Tasha Howe at the Humboldt State University in California is conducting a study, and, if accepted, the results will be presented at the APA 2005 convention.

APA encourages psychologists to participate in the *ACT Against Violence Program* by promoting the media campaign and educational materials in their communities and by participating in the *ACT* training programs. There are many ways for psychologists to be involved with ACT, as advisors, consultants for specific projects, promoters, or as trained-professionals. Some suggestions include:

- Promote the ACT project in your workplace and community: Use ACT publications and booklets, the ACT TV PSA CD ROM and the 'ACT in the Community' 8-minute CD ROM to spread the word about the pro gram and the importance of early prevention.
- Encourage your local or state psychological association to bring ACT to your community: they can do that by promoting ACT in newsletters and conferences and by sponsoring presentations to introduce ACT to their members.
- Encourage the local media to promote early violence prevention: volun teer to be interviewed, identify experts for the local media, and persuade the media to create feature stories and programs on early violence pre vention, and to air the program PSA.
- Become an ACT Community Coordinator: apply for the ACT Program annual 3-day workshop; visit regularly the ACT Web site for informa tion.

Making a difference in such a complex problem as violence prevention requires a sustained effort, and APA continues to pursue support for expansion and refinement of this combination of a nationwide mass media campaign and training efforts. For more information about the ACT Against Violence Program contact Julia Silva at the APA Public Interest Directorate at 202-336-5817 or by e-mail at jsilva@apa.org. Or visit the ACT Web site at www.actagainstvio-lence.org to get additional information and to download or order ACT materials and publications.

References

Bandura, A. (1973). Aggression: A social learning analysis. Oxford, England: Prentice-Hall.

Eron, L. D., Gentry, J. H., & Schlegel, P. (Eds.)(1994). Reason to hope: A psychosocial perspective on violence & youth. Washington, DC: American Psychological Association.

Kumpfer, K. L., & Alvarado, R. (2003). Family-strengthening approaches for the prevention of youth problem behaviors. *American Psychologist, 58*(6-7), Jun-Jul 2003. Special issue: Prevention that works for children and youth. pp. 457-465.

Thornton, T. N., Craft, C. A., Dahlberg, L. L., Lynch, B. S., & Baer, K. (2002). *Best practices of youth violence prevention: A sourcebook for community action.* Atlanta, GA: Division of Violence Prevention, National Center for Injury Prevention and Control, Centers for Disease Control and Prevention.

Parent Development Theory: Understanding Parents, Parenting Perceptions and Parenting Behaviors

Barbara A. Mowder
Psychology Department, Pace University

This article discusses the Parent Development Theory (PDT). Developed over a decade ago, the PDT is a useful theoretical perspective for understanding individuals' parenting perceptions and behaviors. Closely aligned with both social learning and cognitive developmental theories, the PDT posits how individuals construct and modify their parenting point of views over time. More specifically, parenting is viewed as a social role which includes a specific group of individuals called parents, involved in a parent-child dyadic relationship, performing behaviors associated with the parental role. Research associated with the PDT reveals that individuals tend to perceive the parent role as including six primary characteristics: bonding, discipline, education, general welfare and protection, responsivity, and sensitivity. While most individuals view these characteristics as important components of parenting, the relative weighting in terms of importance and frequency varies developmentally. That is, what a parent does in terms of parenting an infant differs from parenting children at other child developmental points in time. This theory is not only useful in terms of understanding and working with parents, but also for exploring parental similarities and differences (e.g., cultural) as well as child development outcomes (e.g., social development).

For the importance of parenting, with the long-term implications for children, families, and society, there is precious little psychological theory specifically on parents and parent development. And, while there are many parent education programs available and certainly substantial research on parents (e.g., Baurmind, 1975, 1991), none are based on an overall theoretical model regarding who parents are and how they develop in relation to the parenting role. This article provides a theoretical framework, the Parent Development Theory (PDT) to assist professionals in organizing their thinking, practice, and research regarding parenting.

Originally called the Parent Role Development Theory (PRDT), the PDT considers parenting by examining the important social role which parents play (Mowder, 1991, 1993, 1997). The parent role is important to understand since it is through this role that individuals perceive what parenting involves and consequently parent children. At various points on any given day, individuals perform other social roles, such as being a friend, teacher or learner, employer or employee. But when individuals interact with their children, they are performing the role of being a parent. Therefore, the PDT defines who parents are, examines the parent role individuals play, clarifies how parents and parenting develop and change over time, and explains how the parent role relates to parenting activities.

The parent role is one key to understanding parents since the role is performed by individuals who create the role as well as respond to role demands (Mowder, Harvey, Moy, & Pedro, 1995). The parent role is partially an individual creation in that people conceptualize parenting based on their own prior experiences in a parent-child relationship, their thoughts and feelings about being a parent, and their child rearing expertise and understanding. But while part of the role is individually thought about, shaped, and refined, other aspects are externally imposed, like legal requirements, in socially well-developed countries, regarding children's protection and welfare.

Parents' perceptions of their role are not only affected by their own developmental experiences, changes, and needs, but also by their changing, growing, developing child. For example, children need continuous care as infants, but as they grow their parental needs change. Thus, parents of infants spend a good deal of time tending to their children by feeding, diapering, cuddling, and holding. As infants become toddlers and then preschoolers, their developmental needs change and parents increasingly focus their efforts on encouraging, guiding, and supervising child exploration. Parental awareness of their child's developmental changes and corresponding needs, not to mention each child's unique characteristics, is tempered by the on going yet evolving parent-child relationship. For instance, family dynamics such as spousal or partner conflict over issues such as child-rearing can affect parents' interactions with their children as well as their parenting perceptions. In addition, the broader social-cultural context also influences parents' views of their parenting role; parents' religious orientation, for example, potentially affects parents' perceptions of their role as well as associated parenting activities (Levine, 2003).

The PDT addresses the issue of parenting by examining how parents, their parent role perceptions, and consequent parenting shifts and changes over time as parents adjust and respond to their own experience, their children, the parent-child relationship, family dynamics, and the social-cultural milieu. Therefore, the PDT is a resource for child developmentalists, counselors, psychologists, social workers, teachers, and other child-oriented professionals who seek to understand parents and parenting, especially in relation to children's growth and development.

Relevance of Theory for Child Oriented Professionals

Much of the most significant work child-oriented practitioners, such as counselors, psychologists, and social workers, do include parents (Wise, 1995). Indeed, if services like assessments and interventions are to be appropriate and meaningful, professionals must work with parents so that, for instance, evaluations are thorough, thoughtful, and complete. If parents are involved, full participants in practitioners' work with children, psychological services have the potential to facilitate children's growth and development (Christenson, Rounds, & Gorney, 1992). In order to work with parents, however, psychologists, as well as other professionals including educators, need to appreciate the complexity of the parent role. For it is through the parent role that parents interact with their children, not to mention the professionals serving them both. In other words, parents are not simply older individuals interacting with a younger one, rather they are people who recognize, assume, and perform the social role of being a parent (Mowder, 1997). Therefore, they relate to their children the way they conceptualize what it means to be a parent and typically act according to those parenting beliefs (Mowder, 2000).

For professionals who work with and provide services to children and their parents, there needs to be an understanding and appreciation of what it means to be a parent. If such an awareness is lacking on the part of service providers, psychological and other child-oriented services are likely to be well intentioned, but probably less than optimal. For example, if a school psychologist makes a recommendation regarding parental behavior without appreciating how this intervention potentially affects other parenting activities, the change in parent behavior may be ineffective and, in fact, problematic in terms of meeting the child's needs (Stiller, 1992).

Despite the importance of parenting, there is limited research on the parent role or parent role characteristics. In other words, while researchers as well as practitioners appreciate that parents are important in children's lives (Barnard & Martell, 1995; Belsky, Crnic, & Woodworth, 1995) and play a key role in children's development (Grusec, Goodnow, & Kuczynski, 2000; Kochanska, 1997; Murphey, 1992), there is a lack of research and writing on exactly what difference practitioners' findings and recommendations make in terms of what parents think about and do relative to their children. Essentially, the issue is, based on psychologists' and educators' findings and subsequent recommendations, what are parents to consider and accomplish differently than they are already doing relative to their children? In other words, how are parents to conceptualize their interactions with their child and behave differently based on what the practitioner recommends? These are key questions in terms of psychological and other child-oriented services, particularly consultation services, since it is anticipated that changes will result from the practitioner's recommendations (Turiano, 2001).

Parent Development Theory

One solution to this problem is the development of the Parent Role Development Theory (PRDT) (Mowder, 1991, 1993, 2000; Mowder et al., 1995), now called the Parent Development Theory (PDT). This theory provides a framework for viewing parents as individuals who acknowledge, accept, and perform the parent role (Mowder, 1997). Viewing parents from this perspective is helpful since being a parent does not simply involve the rather singular biological function of procreation; more significantly, parenting involves the on-going process of carrying out behaviors associated with a specific social role. Indeed, social roles are typically defined as involving an interaction between two individuals, with each one behaving according to that socially recognized role (Bonney, Kelley, & Levant, 1999; Saks & Krupat, 1988; Shonkoff & Meisels, 2000). Thus, social roles require at least two individuals involved in an interaction in which the parties acknowledge their respective roles, are known by society as having the role, and perform behaviors associated with that role. In the case of parents, there are at least two individuals, one a parent and one a child, each of whom is typically involved in a parent-child interaction. Each party is recognized by society as holding that role, and each performs socially acknowledged, role-related activities. With regard to parents, their activities are referred to as parenting (Bard, 1995; Baumrind, 1991; Bower-Russa, Knutson & Wineberger, 2001).

More specifically, in the case of parents, there is always a social interaction in that parents are only parents in the context of a parent-child interaction. In fact, one is only a parent if there is a child that one is parenting. Parenting is also a social role in that societies and cultures recognize individuals as parents (Cole, 1999), and there are behaviors which are associated with and expected of humans (Parke & Buriel, 1998), as well as other primates (Bard, 1995), who hold this designation. Indeed, if socially recognized and anticipated parenting behaviors are not performed, societies typically have social agencies, such as Child Protective Services, which step in and assure that someone else provides the requisite child-related activities (Brassard, Hart, & Hardy, 2000; Pagliocca, Melton, Weisz, & Lyons, 1995). Thus, being a parent involves a socially recognized role, occupied by a group of individuals known as parents, for which specific behaviors are associated. Parenting is a role which is continuous in nature, consistent with the life-long fluctuating demands of a parent-child relationship, and only ceases once there is no longer a parent and a child in that relationship (e.g., death of one of the parties, termination of parental rights) (Mowder, 2002; Mowder et al., 1995).

The PDT not only provides a theoretical framework for considering the parent role, the theory also posits a developmental model in which individual conceptualizations of the parent role shift and change over time (Mowder et al., 1995). Relying primarily on a cognitive-behavioral perspective, Mowder (1997) asserts that early in life, young children begin to appreciate social roles. Young children recognize that parents have a special relationship with their children and parents behave in a particular way; indeed, they see that there are some commonalities among parents in terms of how they relate to and behave toward their children. In fact, research reveals that young children readily describe what parents do (Lessuck-Namer, 1997). Over time, individuals' cognitions or schemata relative to the parent role develop and become more refined (Donnelly, 1992) with increased individual, family, and other social and cultural experiences. These parenting cognitions continue to develop over the life span, regardless of whether individuals themselves become parents. For those who do become parents, the parenting cognitions inform parenting behaviors; that is, parents do not parent in a vacuum, rather parenting behaviors emerge as a result of individuals' own life experiences (including being a child in a parent-child relationship), and, more specifically, their developing parenting cognitions (Mowder, 1991, 2000).

Thus, the PDT provides a view of parenting in which individuals develop their own unique views of what being a parent means. Moreover, parenting cognitions are subject to change over the life span. The factors which affect parenting cognitions include the individuals' own experiences over time, as well as individual personality, education, and other factors (Donnelly, 1992; Mowder, 1993). The parent role cognitions, however, also change as a result of becoming a parent and being involved in a parent-child relationship (Mowder et al., 1995; Stiller, 1992). Not only is the relationship the individual establishes with her/his child relevant, but the child's individual characteristics and specific needs also play a role in influencing and affecting parenting perspectives (Mowder et al., 1995). For example, if an individual has a child who is especially ill or has special education needs, the parent necessarily needs to adjust her/his thinking about what it means to be a parent, accommodating their perceptions to the child's specific developmental needs (Sperling, 2003; Stiller, 1992).

While the parent, child, and their unique parent-child relationship contribute to the parent's view of parenting, there are other factors which also impact the individual parent's perception and refinement of her/his role. More specifically, family dynamics, which might include the individual's spouse, significant other, or partner, other children in the family, and/or extended family members, also affect individuals' perceptions and execution of their parent role. Finally, the social and cultural context in which the individual is living also influences parenting perspectives (Levine, 2003; Mosley-Howard, 1995). What is considered appropriate parenting in one culture, or social situation, for instance, is not necessarily appropriate in another (Shum, 1996). Thus, an individual's view of parenting, at any point in time, is likely to be influenced not only by the individual who is the parent and their own unique background, characteristics, and experiences, but also the child and the child's individual factors such as age, gender, personality, and special needs. In addition, the individual's own, specific parent-child relationship, family dynamics, and social-cultural factors all contribute to an individual's view of parenting (Mowder et al., 1995).

More likely than not, over time, and consistent with other developing cognitions, individuals' parenting perceptions have some level of stability, but are also subject to change. Further, parenting cognitions have a direct, though not a one-to-one correspondence, with parenting behavior. That is, parents tend to parent, or behave toward their children, in a way which is consistent with their views about what is important to do as a parent (Fagot, 1995; Fox & Brice, 2001). There is not always a perfect correspondence between parenting perspectives and parenting behaviors due to any number of issues, such as specific circumstances, individual factors, and so on. Nonetheless, an understanding of how individuals view their parental role is a significant contributor to what and how frequently parenting tasks are performed (Mowder, 2000).

Thus, the PDT is a useful theoretical framework from which to examine individual parenting perspectives. The theory also assists child-oriented practitioners to understand how the individuals they are working with may view parenting from their own unique, specific point of view, which may differ from the practitioner's own perspective (Lawrence, 1995) and, further, provides a way to consider what parents might need to think about and do differently regarding meeting their child's needs. At a more global level, this theory provides one of only a very few models for developing theoretically based programs for parent education, as well as informing and conducting research regarding parent-child relations and child-oriented psychological services. Thus, the PDT has the potential to inform practitioners, program developers, and researchers.

Parent Role Characteristics

Extensive research (e.g., Clifford, 2004; Donnelly, 1992; Mowder, 1991; Mowder, 2000; Mowder et al., 1995; Mowder, Harvey, Pedro, Rossen, & Moy, 1993; Turiano, 2001), over a significant period of time, provides specific parent role characteristics, definitions, and key descriptors. Thus, the six primary characteristics, which emerge from parents regarding their parent role, are bonding, discipline, education, general welfare and protection, responsivity, and sensitivity. Indeed, this research data is consistent with current research on parents (e.g., Bonney et al., 1999; Bower-Russa et al., 2001; Brazelton, 1992; Coley & Chase-Lansdale, 1999; Day, Evans, & Lamb, 1998; Doherty, Kouneski, & Erickson, 1998; Fox & Brice, 2001; Goldberg, Grusec, & Jenkins, 1999; Pleck & Pleck, 1997, Van den Boom, 1997).

Thus, briefly presented, the specific parent role characteristics included in the PDT are as follows:

1. *Bonding* refers to the affection, love, and regard parents feel and display toward their children. This term is used to characterize the positive affect of the parent toward the child, while the corresponding term used to describe the affect of children toward their parents is referred to as attachment (Bell & Richard, 2000; Bowlby, 1988).

2. *Discipline* refers to parents setting limits for their children and assuring that the limits are responded and adhered to. This parenting dimension has sometimes been referred to as permissive versus restrictive parenting (Baumrind, 1975, 1991). In general, discipline involves indications of setting limits or establishing rules, and specific parental responses to child behavior (Gralinski & Kipp, 1993).

3. *Education* is the parental transmission of information in order to inform children. This parenting characteristic includes educating, guiding, and teaching children (Chase-Lansdale, Wakschlag & Brooks-Gunn, 1995). Examples of education include activities such as advising, being a role model, counseling, preparing and showing by example.

4. *General Welfare and Protection* means that parents assure that their children are protected from harm and that children's general needs, such as adequate clothing, food, shelter, temperature, and water are met. Indications of general welfare and protection include, for instance, assuring safety and a healthy environment and being a breadwinner and provider.

5. *Responsivity* means the extent to which parents respond to their children. This means that a parent, for instance, hears, sees, or in some other way perceives that the child needs something and the parent makes a response to the child's call for assistance. Exhibiting responsivity includes, for example, helping, assisting, bringing up, encouraging, and supporting (other than in a general welfare and protection sense) children (e.g., Field, 1990).

6. *Sensitivity* refers to the ability of the parent to discern what the child is communicating and matching the parent response to the child's need. In other words, sensitivity includes a sense of accuracy with which parents understand and respond to their children. Sensitivity includes, for example, indications of respecting, understanding, comforting, and responding to a child's specific need (e.g., DeWolff & van Ijzendoorn, 1997; Lamb, Hwang, Ketterlinus, & Fracasso, 1999).

These parent role characteristics are not mutually exclusive and, furthermore, can be reconfigured to represent other factors, such as caring. Indeed, Turiano (2001) examined a large data set, albeit from a specific geographic area, and found many references to caring, consistent with prior research in this area (Bell & Richard, 2000; Benner & Wrubel, 1989; Bosworth, 1995; Chase-Lansdale et al., 1995; Finkenauer & Meeus, 2000; Noblit, Rogers, & McCadden, 1995). However, her research reveals that caring, in terms of parenting, undoubtedly represents some combination of parent role characteristics (i.e., bonding, discipline, education, general welfare and protection, responsivity, and sensitivity) rather than offering a distinct parenting variable.

What Parenting Is

On-going parenting, in contrast to the biological parent role, represents a continuous set of child rearing behaviors performed by a parent in the context of a parent-child relationship. This on-going, continuous, and long-term set of parent behaviors, is social in nature as the behaviors are part of a social interaction (i.e., between parent and child) and are performed within a social context (i.e., the family, community, and culture) (Parke & Buriel, 1998). Essentially, parenting is the performance or acting out of the social parent role. For instance, when Juanita and Ben feed, clothe, and shelter their children they are parenting, and when they love, guide, and discipline, they are also performing the social role of being a parent.

Who Is Involved in Parenting?

Those who perform on-going parenting activities or the social parent role are parents and even though parents vary considerably on a variety of characteristics, such as age, biological contribution to the conception of the child, and cultural backgrounds, they share an important set of qualities. To varying degrees, this group of individuals recognize, accept, and perform the parent role and individually they are typically recognized in their social milieu as parents of specific children (Mowder, 1997).

Therefore, there are a number of theoretical assumptions related to who is involved in parenting. First, individual parents need to understand that there is such a role as that of being a parent. Indeed, research reveals that even young children are capable of appreciating that there is a group of individuals who are referred to as parents, that parents are part of a relationship (i.e., the parent-child relationship), and that there are behaviors associated with those who are parents (Lessuck-Namer, 1996). Second, parents are individuals who accept the role by identifying themselves as parents, and, third, parents parent by acting according to their view of the parent role. Finally, parents are recognized socially as the parent in a particular parent-child relationship. In other words, people realize they are parents and that there are expectations associated with being a parent, behave differently as a result, and are acknowledged by others as parents.

Individuals are only parents if there is a child for them to parent. The term child is used to designate anyone, regardless of age, to whom an individual is a parent. The term child, therefore, refers to an individual within a parent-child relationship who is the recipient of parenting behaviors. For example, Rose Anne and Jesus are the parents of their children, but they are the children of their parents in another set of parent-child relationships. This use of the term, child, differs from the customary references to anyone who is between birth and eighteen years of age. That age-related child designation usually refers to an individual's developmental, legal, and social status. Within the parent-child relationship, however, the term child means one who performs the social role of being a child. That role includes receiving and responding to parenting, as well as interacting within the parent-child relationship, regardless of the child's age as calculated in years (Mowder, 2000, 2002).

Children have a variety of characteristics which often mirror those of parents. They have different abilities and skills, emotional development, and personalities and temperament. For instance, they have their own preferences and tastes, and form their own social relationships. Like parents, children often acquire a range of diverse social roles such as friend, grandchild, and student. Ultimately, each child is unique, bringing their own individual characteristics to the parent-child and other relationships. Children's characteristics, including for instance age, gender, and temperament, influence how others respond to them (Dumas, LaFreniere, & Serketich, 1995; Stiller, 1992). The attractive, easygoing, happy child, for example, usually brings forth smiles and pleasant words from others, while the difficult child may cause considerable parent frustration. Indeed, Ammerman, Lubetsky, and Drudy (1991) find that child abuse appears to be more frequent with children with disabilities compared with typical children.

Clearly there are other individuals involved in the parenting process. Parents are touched by their family (Lamb et al., 1999; Rubin, Coplan, Nelson, Cheah, & Lagace-Sequin, 1999), community, and social-cultural milieu. From spouses and siblings to teachers and physicians, many individuals as well as social institutions, like the school and church, influence and affect what the parent does (Eccles & Roeser, 1999). For instance, if a child is having difficulty performing in school, the teacher may recommend that the parent help the child with homework in the evening. So rather than playing a game with the child, the responsive parent might supervise homework completion.

Even though there are many individuals ultimately associated with parents and parenting, parenting itself is dyad-specific, meaning that parenting refers exclusively to parent behaviors performed within a particular, unique, two-person parent-child relationship. In other words, while Chandra and Connita are partners and parent their child, Jonas, each one is an individual parent, parenting within their own parent-child relationship, Chandra-Jonas and Connita-Jonas. Each dyad differs somewhat from the other, just as Chandra's and Connita's parenting differs somewhat from each other. Chandra, for instance, may believe that bonding is more important than discipline, while Connita may believe that sensitivity overrides disciplinary activities.

How Parenting Occurs

The interaction or interface factor in the parent-child relationship is the role which each individual plays in relation to the other, within his or her social context. Fermin and Eddie, for example, feed their children Anthony and Josie and take them to school. At the end of the school day, Anthony and Josie wait for one of their parents to pick them up and take them home. Each party in the parent-child relationship relates to the other via their roles as parents and children. Neither role is rigid, rather each changes as parents and children grow and develop. Parent diapering and toileting of babies, for example, give way to other activities as children mature and their needs change, and the parent role shifts in response (Mowder et al., 1995).

Parenting stems from and represents the parent acting out the parent role (Mowder, 1993, 1997, 2000). Parenting is role performance, behavior performed by a specific group of individuals called parents, as a function of their unique parent-child relationship. Thus, if parents see the parent role as primarily disciplinary in nature, assuring that children always behave in specific, acceptable ways, their behavior toward their children will tend to center on that set of issues (Mowder, 2000). On the other hand, if parents see their role as nurturing and primarily as providing love for their children, their behavior will gravitate toward the expression of love and affection toward their children. Whatever an individual parent perceives their role to be, those parenting beliefs or set of assumptions provide the framework for task performance. Thus, parents parent in the context of their parent-child relationship and social-cultural milieu (Cole, 1999), including religious orientation (Levine, 2003) based on their thoughts, feelings, and motivation.

Parenting or parent role performance is complex and does not represent an inborn set of behaviors even though there is evidence that some parenting behavior has an innate origin (Bornstein, 1995). Rather, according to the PDT, parenting is *primarily* learned and reflects parents' education, experience, and knowledge regarding parenting (Mowder, 1993, 1997, 2000). That learning is based primarily on parents' own experiences as a child in a parent-child relationship and observations of others in parenting roles although parents' children, their relationship, family dynamics, and social-cultural factors also influence parenting perceptions (Silverman, 2002).

When Parenting Occurs

Parenting begins as soon as there are a parent and a child in a parent-child relationship. To be sure, parenting perceptions begin early and have been identified in young children (Lessuck-Namer, 1997). But, the actual performance of the parent role does not occur until there are two individuals, a parent and a child, in a parent-child relationship. For instance, this usually occurs when a baby is born or adopted and a parent-child relationship is established (i.e., the parent is recognized in the social setting as the parent). For parenting to begin, of course, parents need to recognize, accept, and perform the social role of being a parent (Mowder, 1997).

Once parenting begins, the role represents an around-the-clock, morning until night, day after day, year after year, lifetime commitment (Mowder, 1993). As long as there are a parent and a child in a parent-child relationship and the parent continues to parent, and is recognized by others as the parent, parenting is occurring. Unlike many other roles, such as vocational roles, which are usually shed at some point in the evening, on weekends, during vacations, or in the course of the lifespan (e.g., retirement), the parent role is usually not set aside until the parent-child relationship ends. The dissolution of the relationship might occur, for instance, with the death of one of the parties or a special circumstance such as the termination of parental rights or the child's emancipation from his/her parent(s).

Even when parents are not directly performing the role of parent (e.g., bonding or disciplining their child), parents assure that their role is being performed in some other way. Thus, there is a distinction between *direct* and *indirect parenting* (Mowder, 2002). *Direct parenting* occurs when parents are directly interacting with their child in the performance of their parent role. In contrast, *indirect parenting,* takes place when parents assure that their parent role activities are being performed, but by someone else (e.g., day-care provider). This distinction is particularly clear in the case of the day care. For example, when the parent is home or elsewhere caring for their child, they are directly assuring that their child's needs are being met by the care and attention they provide. But, when parents work, for example, they may take their children to relatives, baby-sitters, day-care homes, or other day-care facilities assuring that their parent role obligations are being met, even though they themselves are not directly interacting with their child. Thus, day-care represents indirect parenting with the parent making sure that someone is caring for their child, much the way they would if they were present (Mowder, 1993).

In terms of the parent role, parenting ends when there is no longer a parent and child in a parent-child relationship. There are a number of avenues which might lead to the termination of the parenting relationship, such as death of one of the parties, abdication of the parental role though disinterest or incarceration, and formal dissolution of the parent-child relationship (e.g., termination of parental rights). Indeed, some societies legally define when parent responsibilities begin and when they end (Mowder, 2002).

Where Parenting Occurs

Parenting, according to the PDT, occurs wherever individuals are performing either *direct* or *indirect* parent-related activities. In other words, parenting occurs wherever something is being done for the child at the behest of the parent, whether or not the parent is physically present. For example, when parents attend teacher conferences and hire a baby-sitter to care for their child while they are at school, they do so in the context of their parent role. Parenting is occurring both at the school as the parent and the teacher discuss the child's school progress, as well as where the child is while being supervised and cared for while the parent-teacher conference occurs.

In essence, parenting occurs wherever the parent is assuring that the parent role is being performed and their children's needs are being met. The home is the most common place for parenting activities, particularly for parents of young children. But, the beach, church, playground, school, and stores are all examples of places for parenting to happen. These parenting sites represent places and opportunities for both *direct* and *indirect parenting.*

Why There Is Parenting

At the most basic level, parenting occurs as a preservation of the human species and as an assurance of the continuation of societies (Bornstein, 1995). Indeed, parenting is essential in primates (Bard, 1995). Without parenting, children would perish and so, too, would the societies they are born into. So, even though there are considerable variations regarding child-rearing practices throughout the world (Harkness & Super, 1995), no society continues to exist if children are not reared and cared for.

In this context, societies themselves have reason to be concerned that parenting occurs (Pagliocca, Melton, Weisz, & Lyons, 1995). Not only are children necessary for the continuation of the society, but, in addition, they need to be informed and socialized in order to carry on the beliefs, traditions, and values which the society holds. Thus, social concerns are primarily two-fold. In the first place, societies typically share a social responsibility for the children who will mature and take their place in assuring the continuity and continuation of the society. One concern is that if individuals do not parent their young, that society will need to provide those child rearing services (typically at considerable community expense). And, a second concern is that the child rearing provided conforms to prevailing social views. In other words, if a society respects and places a value on a certain behavior, like respecting an individual's property, and yet a parent and/or child destroy someone's possessions, then society will become concerned, involved, and intervene (Pagliocca et al., 1995). Likely, the society's organizational unit concerned with adherence, like social services or judicial systems, is triggered and formal intervention follows.

In addition to social reasons for supporting and monitoring parenting behavior, there are many diverse personal reasons for individuals to parent (Barnard & Martell, 1995). For example, one common parenting reason is the fulfillment of social responsibilities associated with conceiving and bearing a child. But, beyond this basic and often assumed reason to parent, there are many other personal motivations such as wanting to create a relationship with a baby which has opportunities for guiding, loving, and teaching. Parenting can also be viewed as a way to create or cement a relationship between two adults. For instance, if one member fears the loss of the relationship, the individual might reason that a child would be a reason for the couple to stay together. More frequently than not, individual personal reasons for becoming a parent are complex and multifaceted.

One does not have to be a biological parent to desire being a parent and performing the parent role. Indeed, there are vast numbers of individuals and couples who desire being parents but who are unable or uninterested in being biological parents. Like biological parents, these individuals represent a range of reasoning and motivations for becoming parents, including for instance caring for, loving, and providing for another person.

Differences Between Parenting and Procreation

Clearly there are many differences between parenting and procreation. While both activities are, in their own way, complex and related to a single developing child, they are distinctly different functions. Indeed, examining both reveals each one's specific characteristics and related role performance requirements. Based on these differences, there are many implications regarding role performance, including, for instance, who is equipped for each role (e.g., age requirements), to what extent, and what further learning might enhance parenting performance.

Procreation is the physical act of joining a sperm and an egg together to create another biological being. With procreation, the link between the parent and child is direct in that the child has genetic make-up based on both parents' biological contributions (Pagliocca et al., 1995). Thus, with procreation the link between parent and child is clear, unmistakable, and unchangeable. Typically, the biological parents are also the individuals who parent their child; however, this is not necessarily the case. For example, some parents put their children up for adoption, others abandon, abuse, or neglect their children.

Parenting, in contrast to procreation, therefore, is the performance of the social rather than the biological parent role, requiring that individual parents recognize, assume, and perform the parent role (Mowder, 1997). With parenting, the link between the parent and child is not as clear, unmistakable, and unchangeable as with procreation. Parenting responsibilities are neither as clear as they are in procreation, nor are male and female contributions to the task well delineated (Bonney et al., 1999; Coley & Chase-Lansdale, 1999; Phares, 1996). In the first place, there is no consensus on what constitutes parent role responsibility. And, because the role is socially defined and to a large extent subject to individual interpretation, adequate role performance is not spelled out except where abuse and neglect are concerned (Emery & Billings, 1998). As a result, some parenting functions like protecting, feeding, and clothing children are well recognized, while others like bonding and responsivity may not be as obvious and acknowledged as general welfare and safety. For example, a parent may be well prepared financially to assume general welfare responsibilities, but not prepared to meet a child's emotional needs.

In addition to the lack of parent role specificity, who performs the role, in terms of male-female or partnership responsibilities, is also subject to debate. Both mothers and fathers are very influential in their children's development

(Phares, 1996). Research reveals, however, that mothers consistently rate all parent role characteristics, except for discipline, as more important than fathers across all child development stages (Mowder et al., 1995). Even though research suggests that fathers have the ability to parent responsively and sensitively (McHale, Crouter & Bartko, 1991; McHale & Huston, 1984), many do not follow this pattern. With the vast, increasing numbers of women in the work force, the question of male-female parent responsibility and role performance is indeed a contemporary issue (Mowder et al., 1995).

A further difference between procreation and parenting is the assurance of role performance. If there is a child, procreation has "de facto" occurred and the biological parent role was performed (Pagliocca et al., 1995). But given any particular child, there is no such guarantee that the social parent role is performed (unless society steps in to insure the child's well-being). This issue is important to note since the two parent roles lend to some confusion regarding parenting; often, because children have been biologically parented, there tends to be the assumption that they have also been socially parented. But, the occurrence of one does not assure the other; there are examples across cultures and throughout history of children being abandoned, abused, neglected, or otherwise having no one perform the parent role for them.

Finally, the genesis of human beings follows essentially the same format today as it did historically, and even with technological advances in fertility, procreation is still a biological function and occurs in all human, and other animal, cultures throughout the world. Parenting, or performance of the parent role, however, has changed significantly over time and varies considerably from one culture to the next. For example, prior to the twentieth century in western societies, children were viewed as chattel or property, and only recently have many countries begun to recognize children as having rights of their own as exhibited by the recent United Nations International Convention on the Rights of the Child (Brassard et al., 2000).

Summary: Parenting Points of View

Viewing parenting as role performance helps distinguish procreation from on-going parenting, and gives definition to this important activity, but this perspective represents one point of view. The benefits of the PDT are that role performance focuses on what people think about parenting, or conceive parenting to be, and this allows parenting to be accessible, measurable, understandable, and capable of changing. In addition, this cognitive point of view (focusing on what parents think about parenting) provides a point of entry and a coherent framework for considering related parenting phenomena, such as what parent do or how they behave in relation to what it is they think about parenting. And,

60*JECIP*   Volume 1, 2005

finally, while a cognitive framework does not provide a direct relationship between cognition and behavior, this perspective does allow a consideration of behaviors and feelings as they relate to parenting perceptions.

References

Ammerman, R. T. , Lubetsky, M. J. , & Drudy, K. F. (1991). Maltreatment of handicapped children. *Case studies in family violence* (pp. 209-230). New York, NY: Plenum Press.
Bard, K. A. (1995). Parenting in primates. *Handbook of parenting: Volume 2 biology and ecology of parenting* (pp. 27-58). Mahwah, NJ: Lawrence Erlbaum Associates Publishers.
Barnard, K. E., & Martell, L. K. (1995). Mothering. In M. H. Bornstein (Ed.), *Handbook of parenting: Vol. 3: Status and Social Conditions of Parenting* (pp. 3-26). Mahwah, NJ: Erlbaum.
Baumrind, D. (1975). *Early socialization and the discipline controversy.* Morristown, NJ: General Learning Press.
Baumrind, D. (1991). Parenting styles and adolescent development. In R. M. Lerner, A.C. Petersen, & J. Brooks-Gunn (Eds.), *Encyclopedia of adolescence* (Vol. 2, pp. 746-758). New York: Garland Publishing.
Bell, D. C., & Richard, A. J. (2000). Caregiving: The forgotten element in attachment. *Psychological Review, 11*, 69-83.
Belsky, J., Crnic, K., & Woodworth, S. (1995). Personality and parenting: Exploring the mediating role of transient mood and daily hassles. *Journal of Personality, 63*, 905-917.
Benner, P., & Wrubel, J. (1989). *Primacy of Caring.* Menlo Park, CA: Addison-Wesley Publishing Co.
Bonney, J. F., Kelley, M. L., & Levant, R. F. (1999). A model of fathers' behavioral involvement in child care in dual-earner families. *Journal of Family Psychology, 13*, 401-415.
Bornstein, M. H. (Ed.) (1995). *Handbook of parenting: Volume 1 children and parenting.* Mahwah, NJ: Lawrence Erlbaum Associates, Publishers.
Bosworth, K. (1995). Caring for others and being cared for. *Phi Delta Kappa, 76*, 675-679.
Bower-Russa, M. E., Knutson, J. F., & Wineberger, A. (2001). Disciplinary history, adult disciplinary attitudes, and risk for abusive parenting. *Journal of Community Psychology, 29*, 219-240.
Bowlby, J. (1988). *A secure base: Parent-child attachment and healthy human development.* New York: Basic Books.

Brassard, M. R., Hart, S. N., & Hardy, D. B. (2000). Psychological and emotional abuse of children. In R. T. Ammerman & M. Hersen (Eds.), *Case studies in family violence (2nd ed.) (pp. 293-319).* Dordrecht, Netherlands: Kluwer Academic Publishers.

Brazelton, T. B. (1992). *On becoming a family: The growth of attachment before and after birth.* New York: Dell.

Chase-Lansdale, P. L., Wakschlag, L. S., & Brooks-Gunn, J. (1995). A psychological perspective on the development of caring in children and youth: The role of the family. *Journal of Adolescence, 18*, 515-556.

Christenson, S. L., Rounds, T., & Gorney, D. (1992). Family factors and student achievement: An avenue to increase students' success. *School Psychology Quarterly, 7,* 178-206.

Clifford, M.E. (2004). Late adolescents' and young adults' perceptions of the parent role. (Doctoral dissertation, Pace University-New York City, 2004), *Dissertation Abstracts International, 65,* 1576.

Cole, M. (1999). Culture in development. In M. H. Bornstein & M.E. Lamb, *Developmental psychology: An advanced textbook* (pp. 73-124). Mahwah, NJ: Lawrence Erlbaum Associates, Inc.

Coley, R. L. & Chase-Lansdale, P. L (1999). Stability and change in paternal involvement among urban African-American fathers. *Psychotherapy, 13*, 416-435.

Day, R., Evans, V. J., & Lamb, M. (1998). Social fatherhood and paternal involvement: Conceptual, data, and policymaking issues. In the Department of Health and Human Services (Eds.), *Nurturing Fatherhood: Improving data and research on male fertility, family formation and fatherhood* (DHHS Publication. Chapter 4). Washington, D.C.: U.S. Department of Health and Human Services.

DeWolff, M. S., & van Ijzendoorn, M. H. (1997). Sensitivity and attachment: A meta-analysis on parental antecedents of infant attachment. *Child Development, 68*, 571-591.

Doherty, W. J., Kouneski, E. F., & Erickson, M. F. (1998). Responsible fathering: An overview and conceptual framework. *Journal of Marriage and the Family, 60*, 227-292.

Donnelly, L. (1992). *The parent role as perceived by preadolescents.* Unpublished doctoral dissertation, Pace University, New York City.

Dumas, J. E., LaFreniere, P. J., & Serketich, W. J. (1995). "Balance of power": A transactional analysis of control in mother-child dyads involving socially competent, aggressive, and anxious children. *Journal of Abnormal Psychology, 104,* 104-113.

Eccles, J. S., & Roeser, R. W. (1999). School and community influences on human development. In M. H. Bornstein & M. E. Lamb (Eds.), *Developmental psychology: An advanced textbook* (pp. 503-554). Mahwah, NJ: Lawrence Erlbaum Associates, Publishers.

Emery, R. A., & Billings, L. L. (1998). An overview of the nature, causes, and consequences of abusive family relationships. *American Psychologist, 53,* 121-135.

Fagot, B. I. (1995). Parenting boys and girls. In M. H. Bornstein (Ed.), *Handbook of parenting: Volume 1 children and parenting* (pp. 163-183). Mahwah, NJ: Lawrence Erlbaum Associates, Publishers.

Field, T. M. (1990). *Infancy.* Cambridge, MA: Harvard University Press.

Finkenauer, C., & Meeus, W. (2000). How (pro-) social is the caring motive? *Psychological Inquiry, 11,* 100-103.

Fox, G. L., & Brice, C. (2001). Conditional fatherhood: Identity theory and parental investment theory as alternative sources of explanation of fathering. *Journal of Marriage and the Family, 63,* 394-403.

Goldberg, S., Grusec, J. E., & Jenkins, J. M. (1999). Confidence in protection: Arguments for a narrow definition of attachment. *Journal of Family Psychology, 13,* 475-483.

Gralinski, H. J., & Kipp, C. B. (1993). Everyday rules for behavior: Mothers' requests to young children. *Developmental Psychology, 55,* 805-816.

Grusec, J. E., Goodnow, J. J., & Kuczynski, L. (2000). New directions in analyses of parenting contributions to children's acquisition of values. *Child Development, 71,* 205-211.

Harkness, S., & Super, C. (1995). Culture and parenting. In M. H. Bornstein (Ed.), *Handbook of parenting: Volume 2 biology and ecology of parenting* (pp. 211-234). Mahwah, NJ: Lawrence Erlbaum Associates, Publishers.

Kochanska, G. (1997). Multiple pathways to conscience for children with different temperaments: From toddler-hood to age 5. *Developmental Psychology, 33,* 228-240.

Lamb, M.E., Hwang, C. P., Ketterlinus, R. D., & Fracasso, M. P. (1999). Parent-child relationships: Development in the context of the family. In M. H. Bornstein & M.E. Lamb, *Developmental Psychology: An advanced textbook.* Mahwah, NJ: Lawrence Erlbaum Associates.

Lawrence, B. (1995). Educators' perceptions of parental roles. (Doctoral dissertation, Pace University-New York City, 1995), *Dissertation Abstracts International, 56,* 1744.

Lessuck-Namer, C. (1997). Children's perceptions of parental roles. (Doctoral dissertation, Pace University-New York City, 1997), *Dissertation Abstracts International, 58,* 6258.

Levine, J. (2003). The relationship of religious orientation to parenting perceptions and behaviors. (Doctoral dissertation, Pace University-New York
City, 2003), *Dissertation Abstracts International, 64,* 4111.

McHale, S. M., Crouter, A. C., & Bartko, W. T. (1991). Traditional and egali-
tarian patterns of parental involvement: Antecedents, consequences and
temporal rhythms. In R. Lerner & D. Featherman (Eds.), *Advances in
life-span development* (Vol. 9). Hillsdale, NJ: Lawrence Erlbaum
Associates.

McHale, S. M. & Huston, T. L. (1984). Men and women as parents: Sex role ori-
entations, employment, and parental roles. *Child Development, 55,*
1349-1361.

Mosley-Howard, G. S. (1995). Best practices in considering the role of culture.
In A. Thomas & J. Grimes (Eds.), *Best practices in school psychology
III* (pp. 337-345). Washington, D. C.: National Association of School
Psychologists.

Mowder, B. A. (1991, July). Parent role development. Paper presented at the
annual meeting of the International School Psychology Association,
Braga, Portugal.

Mowder, B. A. (1993). Parent role research. *Early Childhood Interests, 8* (3),6.

Mowder, B. A. (1997). Family dynamics. In A. Widerstrom, B. A. Mowder,
& S. R.Sandall (Eds.), *Infant development and risk* (pp. 125-154).
Baltimore: Paul H. Brookes.

Mowder, B. A. (2000, March). Parent role behaviors: Implications for school
psychologists. Paper presented at the annual meeting of the National
Association of School Psychologists, New Orleans.

Mowder, B. A. (2002, March). *Parenting in the United States.* Invited presentation at the Malloy College Symposium On Cross-Cultural Parenting
Issues.

Mowder, B. A., Harvey, V. S., Pedro, M., Rossen, R., & Moy, L. (1993). Parent
Role Questionnaire: Psychometric Qualities. *Psychology in the
Schools, 30,* 205-211.

Mowder, B. A., Harvey, V. S., Moy, L., & Pedro, M. (1995). Parent role characteristics: Parent views and their implications for school psychologists.
Psychology in the Schools, 32, 27-37.

Murphey, D. A. (1992). Constructing the child: Relations between parents'
beliefs and child outcomes. *Developmental Review, 12,* 199-232.

Noblit, G. W., Rogers, D. L., & McCadden, B. M. (1995). In the meantime: The
possibilities of caring. *Phi Delta Kappan, 76,* 680-690.

Pagliocca, P. M., Melton, G. B., Weisz, V., & Lyons, P. M. (1995). Parenting and the law. In M. H. Bornstein (Ed.), *Handbook of parenting: Volume 3 status and social conditions of parenting* (pp. 437-457). Mahwah, NJ: Lawrence Erlbaum Associates, Publishers.

Parke, R. D. & Buriel, R. (1998). Socialization in the family: Ethnic and ecological perspectives. In W. Damon (Ed.), *Handbook of child psychology* (Vol. 3). New York: Wiley.

Phares, V. (1996). *Fathers and developmental psychopathology.* New York: Wiley.

Pleck, E. H., & Pleck, J. H. (1997). Fatherhood ideals in the United States: Historical dimensions. In M. E. Lamb (Ed.), *The role of the father in child development* (3rd ed., pp.33-48). New York: Wiley.

Rubin, K. H., Coplan, R. J., Nelson, L. J., Cheah, C. S. L., & Lagace-Sequin, D. G. (1999). Peer relationships in childhood. In M. H. Bornstein & M. E. Lamb (Eds.), *Developmental psychology: An advanced textbook* (pp. 451-502). Mahwah, NJ: Lawrence Erlbaum Associates, Publishers.

Saks, M. J., & Krupat, E. (1988). *Social psychology and its applications.* New York: Harper and Row.

Shonkoff, J. P., & Meisels, S. J. (2000). *Handbook of early childhood intervention.* Cambridge: Cambridge University Press.

Shum, L. M. (1997). A study of the parent role: The Chinese-American perspective. (Doctoral dissertation, Pace University-New York City, 1997), *Dissertation Abstracts International, 57,* 7237.

Silverman, L. (2004). The relationship of parenting beliefs and behaviors to child and adolescent social skills and problem behaviors. (Doctoral dissertation, Pace University-New York City, 2004), *Dissertation Abstracts International, 65, 3773.*

Sperling, S. (2003). Parenting perceptions and behaviors of preschool parents. (Doctoral dissertation, Pace University-New York City, 2003), *Dissertation Abstracts International, 64,* 975.

Stiller, J. (1992*).* Perceptions of parental roles held by adoptive parents of special needs children. (Doctoral dissertation, Pace University-New York City, 1992), *Dissertation Abstracts International, 54, 5987.*

Turiano, R. A. (2001). Parent role characteristics: Parents' perceptions of their parent role. (Doctoral dissertation, Pace University-New York City, 2001), *Dissertation Abstracts International, 62, 2995.*

Van den Boom, D. C. (1997). Sensitivity and attachment: Next steps for developmentalists. *Child Development, 64,* 592-594.

Wise, P. S. (1995). Communicating with parents. In A. Thomas & J. Grimes (Eds.), *Best practices in school psychology III* (pp. 279-287). Washington, D. C.: National Association of School Psychologists.

Parental Perceptions and Preschoolers with Disabilities: An Investigation of Response Variations

Pamela E. Guess
University of Tennessee at Chattanooga

Collaboration represents the means by which family-centered early intervention services emerge in relation to a child with a disability. As with any relationship, the interactions between parents and early intervention service providers are influenced by numerous variables. Sensitivity to family uniqueness, empathic communications, and positive beliefs about the child with the disability and the family are among the documented factors contributing to constructive interactions (Dinnebeil & Rule, 1994). In contrast, a factor impeding productive relationships relates to stereotypical assumptions by the early intervention professional. While parental response research supports varying reactions to a child with a disability, some investigations suggest that professionals may use the more stereotypical belief that parents typically experience heightened distress. The purpose of this study was to document response variations through comparing groups of parents of preschoolers with disabilities to a control group. In addition to more traditional analyses, distributions of responses and normative comparisons were employed. Results supported a range of response in all three groups of parents. Implications for early intervention professionals and approach to family assessments are discussed.

Family-centered services represent a philosophical hallmark in early childhood intervention. Advancing from earlier child-centered, professional-driven notions, legislative mandates emphasizing full family involvement via the Individuals with Disabilities Education Act (IDEA) have been embraced by the early intervention field. Practices involving identification of family strengths, emphasizing family choice regarding services, addressing child and family

College of Health, Education, and Applied Professional Studies, Department 4154, 615 McCallie Avenue, Chattanooga, TN 37403. Pamela-Guess@utc.edu needs, and collaborating with families are now advocated in the field of early intervention (Bruder, 2000).

The rationale for this philosophical progression emanates from the basic principle that families play a crucial role in child development. Best practices in early intervention capitalize on family involvement and consider family strengths, priorities, and concerns in assessments and service plans (Childress, 2004). Family-centered services are nurtured through the collaborative relationship between early intervention professionals and families (Dinnebeil, Hale, & Rule, 1999). As described by Bailey et al. (1998), "the essence of a family-centered approach lies in the relationship that exists between parents and professionals" (p. 314).

Variables Influencing Collaboration

A variety of factors contributing to the productivity of the relationship have been identified. Characteristics of early intervention professionals described by parents as significantly impacting interactions have included beliefs about the child with a disability, ability to empathically communicate, and attitudes demonstrated toward the family. Other positive variables include family centeredness and a focus on family strengths (Dinnebeil & Rule, 1994; Dunst, Johanson, Rounds, Trivette, & Hamby, 1992).

McWilliam, Tocci, and Harbin (1998) investigated beliefs and behaviors of service providers that communicate and enhance family centered practice in relationships with parents. One theme that emerged involved the "willingness to orient services to the whole family, rather than just to the child" (p. 213). In addition, positive expectations and sensitivity to families were identified.

While family-centeredness ideals pervade the literature, Bruder (2000) asserts that, in practice, barriers exist to implementation of this philosophy. Perceptions and attitudes were highlighted as a major impediment. Bruder (2000) stated, "the attitudes of those in early intervention who still see themselves as 'expert' and the family as 'client'" (p. 117) perhaps represent the most important obstacle.

Beliefs professionals have about parental responses to a child's disability represent a specific attitude that may impede family-centered practice. Even though family response literature supports varying responses, a common stereotype is that having a child with a disability results in family distress (Beckman, 1991). Some studies have supported distress as evidenced by significant anxiety, depression, and disengagement in comparison to control groups; however, other investigations have discovered positive adaptation, coping, and adjustment (Flaherty & Masters-Glidden, 2000; Judge, 1998; Scorgie & Sobsey, 2000). Variability has also existed in investigations of the relationship between parental stress and child age (Flynt & Wood,1989), severity of disability (Hodapp, Ly, Fidler, & Ricci, 2001; Orr, Cameron, Dobson, & Day, 1993), and type of disability (Cameron, Dobson, & Day, 1991; Hauser-Cram, Warfield, Shonkoff, & Krauss, 2001). Still other inquiries have yielded varying levels of parental stress (Pipp-Siegel, Sedey, Yoshinaga-Itano, 2002; Sirbasku-Cohen, 2001), marital distress (Nelson, Ruch, Jackson, Bloom, & Part, 1992), depression and psychological distress (Dunn, Burbine, Bowers, & Tantleff-Dunn, 2001), and stress in family relationships (Gray, 2002) within families of children with disabilities. Again, a continuum of response to parenting a child with a disability is implicated given variability of results.

In contrast to response variability indicated above, some investigations suggest that professionals may continue to view families according to the preconceived stress stereotype. For example, Bebko, Konstantareas, and Springer (1987) reported that professionals' ratings of parental stress were significantly higher than parents had rated themselves. In this investigation, parental ratings of stress were compared to ratings from professionals who directly worked with these families of children with autism. While mothers' and fathers' ratings were significantly correlated, suggesting agreement in level of stress associated with various behaviors, professionals consistently rated families as significantly more stressed than mothers and fathers had reported. Bebko et al. (1987) concluded that this discrepancy in ratings may have resulted from the influence of a more traditionally held assumption professionals have of families, i.e., the presence of child with a disability unequivocally results in heightened stress.

Similar findings were suggested by Nelson et al. (1992) in a study of "climate" in families of children with disabilities. Results from the Family Environment Scale (FES) administered to all family members in intact families with a child with a disability indicated that scores on Cohesion and Achievement-Orientation subscales were significantly higher ($p < .05$) than the FES norm group. However, in contrast, family interviewers (i.e., social workers) rated the families in this study as having significant conflict and control problems. In essence, ratings by non-family members reflected more problems than that reported by the family members, themselves.

Nelson et al. (1992) emphasized the clinical implications of having inaccurate and erroneous knowledge of families. Unless practitioners validate their own perceptions with actual family reports of functioning, it is possible that unchecked biases will result in the identification of problems when they may not exist. If utilizing an assumption of inevitable psychological distress, professionals may imply to families that "children without disabilities are easy to raise and children with disabilities are a burden" (Turnbull & Turnbull, 1986, p. 111).

Moving Beyond the Stereotype

Family response investigations have recently shifted toward a strengths-based, coping approach to understanding families (Ferguson, 2002). Findings from these studies represent an influential source of information for expanding perceptions about families. Augmenting traditional research through comparison of parents of children with disabilities to families of children without disabilities represents another method. That is, comparisons of parents of children with disabilities to control groups as well as making normative comparisons may yield a broader understanding (Innocenti, Huh, & Boyce, 1992). Instead of relying solely on parents of children without disabilities as the "norm", including normative based comparisons may yield a more comprehensive understanding of response.

To document the range of parental response, the present investigation was designed to compare parents of preschoolers with mental retardation, parents of children with autism, and parents of children without disabilities on a measure of parental stress. Statistical comparisons of the three groups were completed relative to score distributions; descriptive information and clinically relevant comparisons were also provided. The intent of these analyses was to add to existing literature in documenting a continuum of response in a variety of ways. Demonstration of response heterogeneity in all three groups was hypothesized. Inherently embedded in this hypothesis is the hope that further investigations utilizing traditional and supplemental analyses may offer alternative ways of conceptualizing the range of parental responses.

Method

Participants

Fifty-three parents served as participants for this study; 18 of the participants were parents of children with mental retardation, 17 were parents of children with autism, and 18 were parents of children without disabilities. Parents of children with disabilities were identified from records of enrollees from one public and two private special education preschool programs. For the control group, parents of children from Head Start programs and from two regular preschool programs were identified. Based on criteria provided by the investigator, school directors provided eligible parents (those who met inclusion criteria) with information to request participation. To prevent bias in parent recruitment, directors were given only a general description of the study, i.e., the study focused on parenting preschoolers. Potential participants were excluded if they had any chronic or terminal illnesses, psychoses, or brain injury. Exclusionary criteria were established to eliminate the possible influence of an additional prolonged stressor the parents may have experienced. The total return rate from all eligible parents was 55%.

Responses from mothers and fathers were included in this investigation. Mothers represented the largest proportion of respondents (77%). The total sample ranged in age from 20 to 53 years ($M = 33.23$, $SD = 7.96$); 60% were Caucasian and 38% were African-American. The sample consisted predominantly of mothers (77%) who were married (75%). The majority of participants were employed (60%) with annual household incomes as follows: $0 - $10,000 = 28%, $20,000 - $29,999 = 43%, $30,000 - $39,999 = 9%, $40,000 - $ 49,999 = 11%, and $50,000 or more = 9%. Most participants were either high school graduates (49%) or college graduates (26%). For some families, the preschooler was the only child in the family (21%); others had two (47%), three (19%), or four (13%) children. The majority of preschoolers were male (68%) and all ranged in age from 3 years to 6 years of age ($M = 4$ years, 11 months; $SD = 13.77$ months). With the exception of somewhat higher income and educational levels, total parent sample demographics approximated that of current census information. Each Group, as described below, included participants from both urban and suburban settings.

Parents of children between ages three and six who had been identified as mentally retarded according to state special education criteria comprised Group One. Criteria for special education eligibility for mental retardation included deficits in intellectual functioning and adaptive behavior skills, falling more than two standard deviations below average. Only children functioning within the mild to moderate range of retardation (Intelligence Quotient, $45 - 70$) and without physical or health impairments were included to eliminate the influence of other disabilities (Flynt & Wood, 1989). The investigator reviewed formal assessment information to identify eligible participants for Group One.

Group Two was comprised of parents of preschoolers with a diagnosis of autism according to state criteria; for inclusion, the child could have only a diagnosis of autism and no additional diagnoses such as mental retardation. State criteria for autism included documentation of qualitative impairments in social, language, and behavioral functioning. This group of parents has been identified in some literature as having the greatest levels of stress in response to children with disabilities (Hoppes & Harris, 1990; Wolf, Noh, Fisman, & Speechly, 1989).

Group Three consisted of parents of children with no disability. School staff screened potential participants in this control group to ensure that the child had no disabilities present, had not been referred for an evaluation due to suspected disability, nor did the child's siblings have a disability. This screening involved review of current information routinely collected from the parents. In all regular preschool centers, it was noted by the investigator that ongoing child find efforts were completed such that staff in these settings were quite familiar with criteria for evaluation referral for area school systems.

To confirm equivalence of parent groups, demographics were compared. Groups were not significantly different in regard to parental age, income, or family structure (either a one- or two- parent family). Differences identified included Group One having a significantly lower educational level, F (2, 50) = 3.49, p = .03, and more children in the home, F (2, 50) = 5.54, p = .006. Also, their preschoolers were significantly older than those of the other two groups, F (2,50) = 5.54, p =.006.   Group Two was comprised of significantly more fathers, F (2, 50) = 4.78, p = .01. Refer to Table 1 for specific information about child age range and gender for the three groups.

Table 1: Demographic Characteristics of Preschoolers

	Group One (MR) (n=18)	Group Two (A) (n=17)	Group Three (ND) (n=18)
Age Range	46-80	36-80	39-69
	(M=65.8)[a]	(M=56.5)	(M=51.7)
Males	10	13	12
Females	8	4	6

[a] p < .01, Group One significantly lower.

Measures

Each subject completed a demographic form and a questionnaire related to parental stress. The completed demographic form provided information about parent age, educational level, income level, family structure, and number of children living in the home. Information about preschooler age, sex, disability, and the presence of any siblings with disabilities was obtained through review of school records by the school directors. Also, questions were included on the demographic form provided by the investigator that asked specifically about siblings and any medical/educational services that they either had or currently received.

Parenting Stress Index (PSI). The *Parenting Stress Index* (PSI; Abidin, 1990), a 101-item questionnaire frequently used in family response research, was completed by participants to provide information about parental perceptions of stress. The instrument was administered to parents in all three groups to obtain information regarding their preschoolers in 13 sub-domains comprising the Child, Parent, and Total Stress Domains. A variety of studies reported by Abidin (1990) indicate significant correlations with instruments such as the *Beck Depression Inventory*, the *Symptom Checklist-90*, a broader measure of psychological functioning, and the *Questionnaire on Resources and Stress*. Adequate content, construct, concurrent, and predictive validity have also been reported (Abidin, 1990). The instrument was normed with parents of children from one to twelve years of age; recruitment of parents from both public and private school settings from a cross-section of geographic regions was described by Abidin (1990). Extensive information relevant to technical characteristics is provided in the test manual.

The readability index for the PSI was identified as approximately the mid-sixth grade level (6.7) according to Microsoft Word analysis (based on the commonly used Flesch-Kincaid Grade Level measure of readability). This analysis was completed by the investigator by scanning the PSI Test Booklet into Microsoft software.

As defined by Abidin (1990), "The total stress a parent experiences is a function of certain child characteristics, parental characteristics, and situational variables which are directly related to the role of the parent" (p. 71). Parental perceptions are emphasized by the instrument and, according to Abidin (1990), the role of cognitive appraisal in stressful experiences is recognized. The PSI yields a variety of scores including percentiles and clinical cut-off comparisons.

The Total Score from the PSI, the most reliable index of the summary scores that reflects the total stress in the parent-child system (Abidin, 1990), was utilized to provide a measure of parental perceptions of stress in this investigation. The Total Score is based on items from both the Child Domain and the Parent Domain; thus, the Total Score represents a cross-section of parental perceptions about child characteristics and parent characteristics. Subscales utilized for determining the Total score include Depression, Sense of Competence, Restriction of Role (from Parent Domain) and, from the Child Domain, Adaptability, Demandingness and Reinforces Parent. Alpha reliabilities for the PSI used with participants in this study were as follows: Total Score = .92, Child

Domain=.82, and Parent Domain=.90; all are comparable to the reliability coefficients reported by Abidin (1990).

Results

Results from the PSI were analyzed in a variety of ways to investigate the hypothesis that heterogeneity of response would be demonstrated. First, an analysis of the number of parents in all three groups scoring above and below the PSI mean was completed. A focus on the range of individual scores was emphasized via the use of chi-square analysis based on nominal categorization of each parent's score. The range of scores is often obscured in investigations based on standard group mean comparisons.

Total Stress

To determine if differences existed in the distribution of scores between groups, a 2 X 3 chi-square analysis was performed with the PSI Total Score, the score that represented the overall level of stress a parent reported (Abidin, 1990). An expectancy table was developed from individual scores within and across groups from the number of parents with high and low scores. Parents' scores were grouped by their PSI Total Stress score being above or below the mean and by child condition which consisted of three levels: Group One (MR) – parents of children with mental retardation, Group Two (A) – parents of children with autism, and Group Three (ND)—parents of children with no disability. This analysis, validated for use in family response research, was designed to separate parent groups into subgroups of high and low scorers on the stress measure (Miller, Gordon, Daniele & Diller, 1992; Thompson, Gustafson, Hamlett & Spock, 1992).

Results indicated no significant differences existed between groups, X^2 (2, N = 53) = 1.05, p = .59. That is, in each condition, results revealed variability of scores within each group. In all groups, some parents reported high levels of perceived stress whereas other parents within the same group reported lower stress levels.

Parent Domain and Depression subdomain

Supplemental analyses were completed to determine if significant differences were exhibited on the Parent Domain and the Depression subdomain from the PSI, additional PSI measures sensitive to parental stress. No significant differences between groups were indicated on either scale, the Parent Domain (X^2 (2, N = 53) = .54, p = .76) or Depression (X^2 (2, N = 53) = .24, p = .88). Again, the hypothesis of heterogeneity, or having a distribution of scores, was supported.

Essentially, there were not significantly more parents of children with disabilities who received PSI Total, Parent Domain, or Depression subdomain scores above and below the mean.

Descriptive Data

Variability of response was also analyzed through consideration of the specific range of scores for each group. This descriptive information reflected the large range of variability within all groups. The range between the minimum and maximum scores of the PSI indicated that low and high scores across all groups were obtained. All groups had parents who scored at least one standard deviation below the mean and two standard deviations above the mean on the Total Stress score, the Parent Domain score, and the Depression subdomain. Again, variability of response in all three groups was demonstrated.

Normative Group Comparison

Scores from the three groups on the PSI Total Stress score, the Parent Domain, and the Depression subdomain were compared to scores from the pre-existing norm group (Abidin, 1990). This comparison allowed for consideration of the possible clinical significance of differences relative to a large, normative population. Comparisons indicated that the average scores from all three groups on the Parent Domain and the Depression subdomain fell within one standard deviation from the norm group average. The average Total Stress score for Group One (MR) and Group Three (ND) fell within the average range for the norm group. However, the average Total Stress score for Group Two (A) fell slightly above (5 points) the normative average range. Table 2 presents information on the normative comparisons for the PSI.

Clinical Significance

As the final analysis with PSI results, parents' scores from all three groups were compared using interpretive guidelines (Abidin, 1990). Specifically, the number of parents was identified across the three groups who scored at or above the 80th percentile, the cut-off recommended by the test's author as clinically significant. Table 3 provides information regarding specific frequencies.

Descriptive data indicated that less than half of Group One (MR) and Group Three (ND) had scores above the cut-off on the Total Stress, Parent Domain, and Depression subdomain. Group Two (A) had less than half who scored above the cut-off on the Parent Domain and the Depression subdomain. However, 58.8% of parents scored above the cut-off for the Total stress score.

Table 2: Percent of Scores Above and Below Average for PSI Total Stress, Parent Domain, and Depression.

	Group One (MR) (n = 18) Low/High	Group Two (A) (n=17) Low/High	Group Three (ND) (n=18) Low/High
Total Stress	n = 7/11	4/13	5/13
Parent Domain	n =12/6	11/6	10/8
Depression	n = 8/10	8/9	7/11

Table 3: Numbers of Parents Scoring above the Clinical Score of 80th Percentile on the Parenting Stress Index

	Group One (MR) (n = 18)	Group Two (A) (n=17)	Group Three (ND) (n=18)
Total Stress	7 (38.8%)	10 (58.8%)	7 (38.8%)
Parent Domain	3 (16.6%)	4 (23.5%)	7 (38.8%)
Depression	3 (16.6%)	2 (11.7%)	4 (22.2%)

Discussion

The purpose of this study involved documenting variability in parental response to preschoolers with and without disabilities. Rather than relying on traditional group mean comparisons, analyses of score distributions within groups were completed. These methods were utilized to determine the ways in which parents of preschoolers with mental retardation, autism, and no disability may actually demonstrate similarities. This approach is in contrast to more typical investigations in which differences, based on mean comparisons, are predicted from the outset.

Practical applications of results relate to expanding beliefs and attitudes that professionals may have about families, particularly those of children with disabilities. While individualizing early intervention services based on child and family needs is considered best practice, the gap between research and practice appears to prevent authentic application of this ideal (Bruder, 2000). In fact, investigations comparing parental and professionals' assessments of family stress have yielded higher estimates by the professionals than that reported by families (Bebko et al., 1987, Nelson et al., 1992). Such findings as well as qualitative experiences occur even with the shift toward coping based models and research reflective of variability in response (Bruder, 2000). Thus, stereotypical beliefs related to parenting children with disabilities may be inaccurately imposed on families, contradicting ideals inherent in family-centered practice.

Results from this investigation consistently supported the hypothesis related to variability in a number of ways. First, the distribution of scores in each of the three groups was separated into high and low scorers on the Parenting Stress Index (PSI) Total Stress score; chi-square analyses indicated that the three groups did not demonstrate significant differences in number of parents in each of these respective categories. This same finding was demonstrated on the Parent Domain and the Depression subdomain, PSI measures also sensitive to perceived level of personal stress experienced by the parent. When investigating variability within the three groups from another perspective, minimum to maximum scores, wide score differences were also noted. For the PSI Total Stress, Parent Domain, and Depression subdomain scores, all three groups contained scores falling within one standard deviation below and two standard deviations above average.

Two other analyses with the PSI were completed to examine clinical significance of scores. First, the mean score for each group was compared to the average score for the PSI norm group. With the exception of the Total Stress score for Group Two (A), all group average summary scores fell within one standard deviation of the norm group. For the group of parents of children with autism, the average Total Stress score was just beyond one standard deviation above average. However, this average score is considered clinically significant; this suggests that, as a group, parents of children with autism reported higher than average stress overall. It is noted that ratings of child characteristics, such as adaptability, influence the Total score; given definitive features of autism, it is likely that these behaviorally-related ratings contributed to higher scores. This is consistent with other findings from studies with parents of children with autism who describe behavioral features as particularly stressful (Dunn et al., 2001).

A second analysis related to clinical significance indicated that less than 50% of parents in each of the three groups received elevated scores on the Parent Domain and the Depression subdomain. However, the parents of children with autism reported more clinically elevated Total Stress scores. Again, due to the unique features of autism, it may be that challenges specific to the diagnosis affected the parents' ratings of overall stress.

Practical Implications

Within the climate of family-centered ideals, this investigation reinforces several principles. Foremost, results underscore the imperative for early intervention professionals to consider each family as a unique unit, rather than imposing preconceived notions. As stated by McWilliam et al. (1998), a strategy toward supporting family-centered practices "is checking out families' feelings and reasons before jumping to conclusions" (p. 216). Ultimately, all professionals interacting with families with disabilities must evaluate their views to ensure understanding beyond use of general stereotypes. Results from this investigation obviously indicate that parenting preschoolers, regardless of child condition (i.e., disability or no disability), may be related to parental report of heightened stress.

More comprehensively stated, results support the notion that varying stress levels are reported by parents of preschoolers, regardless of child condition. Therefore, factors other than child condition must also be considered when completing family assessments. As supported by coping based research, other factors such as use of various coping strategies should be considered when assessing parental stress (Guess, 2004; Judge, 1998).

A final implication concerns parents of children with autism. Compared to the other two groups of parents as well as normative comparisons, PSI results suggested that parents of children with autism received clinically significant stress scores. However, these elevations did not appear reflective of personal stress such as depression as much as they were representative of concerns about child factors. While this group of parents has been identified as having heightened stress, it appears necessary to evaluate specific factors that contribute to these reports.

Directions for future research are suggested from this study. Additional investigations that include more detailed descriptions of child characteristics may assist in delineating behaviors – not diagnoses – that parents perceive as stressful. While results from the parents of children with autism suggested relatively increased stress, information about specific child behaviors that may have influenced such scores was not obtained. Another possible child factor not directly considered was intellectual functioning level. While students with diagnoses in addition to autism were not included in Group Two (Autism), the specific intellectual functioning levels of students in this group were not analyzed. No information about cognitive functioning level was obtained for Group Three (No Disability). Examination of this child factor and its possible impact may be helpful to fully understand parental responses, particularly for parents such as those included in Groups Two and Three. Also, time since diagnosis for Groups One and Two was not investigated. Given that temporal aspects of diagnosis may be related to parental response (Orr, Cameron, Dobson, & Day, 1993; Wikler, Wasow, & Hatfield, 1981), considering this factor may be of particular importance for understanding families of children with disabilities. However, while some studies suggest that there is a relationship between timing of diagnosis and stress, others do not support this conclusion (Flynt & Wood, 1989; Wikler, 1986). Further investigation is warranted to provide additional data regarding parental response across time.

Another area for research concerns professional ratings of parental stress. In the broad context of family-centered practice, it is necessary to obtain direct information from professionals about perceptions of stress experienced by the families with whom they work. Comparative studies that involve both family and professional ratings may be of assistance in further sensitizing professionals to response variability. In practice, it may be helpful for early intervention professionals to complete such relative evaluations routinely with themselves and the families with whom they work to monitor match between perceptions.

Sample sizes in the present study represent another consideration. While a wide range of response was demonstrated, the number of parents in each group was limited. Replication of similar analyses with larger samples and with parents of children in other age ranges is necessary to strengthen implications. Also, replication of this study with samples of fathers would be beneficial. In that the sample of parents of children with autism was comprised largely of fathers, obtaining additional information about paternal ratings is recommended. Identification of factors associated with reports of heightened stress in fathers is recommended, in particular. Given that fathers are more rarely included in investigations of parental response (Thompson et al., 1992), additional information is necessary to assist in family assessments that address paternal concerns. Given that number of fathers who participated in this study was relatively smaller than mothers, generalization of results to fathers is limited.

Finally, qualitative analyses with parents that further define themes in professionals' attitudes, particularly as related to parenting a child with a disability, would have significant practical value. Given that numerous factors impact perceived stress level, a more comprehensive investigation including such factors as parental support, financial resources, educational services available, and experiences working with professionals are among a few of the additional factors that merit further investigation. Most importantly, information obtained directly from parental experiences may have the most powerful impact toward narrowing the gap between family-centered ideals and practice for those of us in the early intervention field.

References

Abidin, R. R. (1990). *Parenting stress index (3rd ed.).* Charlottesville, VA: Pediatric Psychology Press.

Guess, P. E. (2004). Parental perceptions of stress and coping: An investigation of parents of preschoolers with and without disabilities. Manuscript submitted for publication.

Bailey, D. B., McWilliam, R. A., Darkes, L. A., Hebbeler, K., Simeonsson, R. J., Spiker, D., & Wagner, M. (1998). Family outcomes in early intervention: A framework for program evaluation and efficacy research. *Exceptional Children, 64,* 313-326.

Bebko, J. M., Konstantareas, M. M., & Springer, J. (1987). Parent and professional evaluations of family stress associated with characteristics of autism. *Journal of Autism and Developmental Disorders, 17,* 565-576.

Beckman, P. J. (1991). Comparison of mothers' and fathers' perceptions of the effect of young children with and without disabilities. *American Journal on Mental Retardation, 95,* 585-595.

Brett, J. (2002). The experience of disability from the perspective of parents of children with profound impairment: Is it time for an alternative model of disability? *Disability and Society, 17,* 825-843.

Bruder, M. B. (2000). Family-centered early intervention: Clarifying our values for the new millennium. *Topics in Early Childhood Education, 20,* 105-135.

Cameron, S. J., Dobson, L. A., & Day, D. M. (1991). Stress in parents of developmentally delayed and non-delayed preschool children. *Canada's Mental Health, 5,* 13-17.

Childress, D. C. (2004). Special instruction and natural environments: Best practices in early intervention. *Infants and Young Children, 17,* 162-176.

Dinnebeil, L. A., Hale, L., & Rule, S. (1999). Early intervention program practices that support collaboration. *Topics in Early Childhood Special Education, 19,* 225-235.

Dinnebeil, L. A. & Rule, S. (1994). Variables that influence collaboration between parents and service coordinators. *Journal of Early Intervention, 18,* 349-361.

Dunn, M. E., Burbine, T., Bowers, C. A., & Tantleff-Dunn, S. (2001). Moderators of stress in parents of children with autism. *Community Mental Health Journal, 37,* 39.

Dunst, C. J., Johanson, C., Rounds, T., Trivette, C. M., & Hamby, D. (1992). Characteristics of parent-professional partnerships. In S. L. Christenson & J. C. Conoley (Eds.), *Home-school collaboration: Enhancing children's academic and social competence* (pp. 157-174). Silver Spring, MD: National Association of School Psychologists.

Ferguson, P. M. (2002). A place in the family: An historical interpretation of research on parental reactions to having a child with a disability. *Journal of Special Education, 36,* 124-132.

Flaherty, E. M., & Masters-Glidden, L. (2000). Positive adjustment in parents rearing children with Down's syndrome. *Early Education and Development, 11,* 407-422.

Flynt, S. W., & Wood, T. A. (1989). Stress and coping of mothers of children with moderate mental retardation. *American Journal of Mental Retardation, 94,* 278-283.

Gray, D. E. (2002). Ten years on: A longitudinal study of families of children with autism. *Journal of Intellectual and Developmental Disability, 27,* 215-222.

Hauser-Cram, P., Warfield, M. E., Shonkoff, J. P., & Krauss, M. W. (2001). Children with disabilities; a longitudinal study of child development and parent well-being. *Monographs of the Society for Research in Child Development, 66(3),* 1-131.

Hodapp, R. M., Ly, T. M., Fidler, D. J., & Ricci, L. A. (2001). Less stress, more rewarding: Parenting children with Down's syndrome. *Parenting: Science and Practice, 1,* 317-337.

Hoppes, K., & Harris, S. L. (1990). Perceptions of child attachment and maternal gratification: Mothers of children with autism and Down's syndrome. *Journal of Clinical Child Psychology, 19,* 365-370.

Innocenti, M. S., Huh, K., & Boyce, G. C. (1993). Families of children with disabilities: Normative data and other considerations on parenting stress. *Topics in Early Childhood Special Education, 12,* 403-427.

Judge, S. L. (1998). Parental coping strategies and strengths in families of young children with disabilities. *Family Relations, 47,* 663.

McWilliam, R. A., Tocci, L., & Harbin, G. L. (1998). Family-centered services: Service providers' discourse and behavior. *Topics in Early Childhood Special Education, 18,* 206-225.

Miller, A. C., Gordon, R. M., Daniele, R. J., & Diller, L. (1992). Stress, appraisal, and coping in mothers of disabled and nondisabled children. *Journal of Pediatric Psychology, 17,* 587-605.

Nelson, M., Ruch, S., Jackson, Z., Bloom, L., & Part, R. (1992). Towards an understanding of families with physically disabled adolescents. *Social Work in Health Care, 17,* 1-25.

Orr, R. R., Cameron, S. J., Dobson, L. A., & Day, D. M. (1993). Age-related changes in stress experienced by families with a child who has developmental delays. *Mental Retardation, 31,* 171-176.

Pipp-Siegel, S., Sedey, A. L., Yoshinaga, & Itano, C. (2002). Predictors of parental stress in mothers of young children with hearing loss. *Journal of Deaf Studies and Deaf Education, 7,* 1-7.

Scorgie, K., & Sobsey, D. (2000). Transformational outcomes associated with parenting children who have disabilities. *Mental Retardation, 38,* 195-206.

Sirbasku-Cohen, S. L. (2001). Parents of children diagnosed with PDD: An examination of family strengths, coping, distress, and efficacy. *Dissertation Abstracts International, Section B, The Sciences and Engineering, 61,* 5006.

Thompson, R. J., Gustafson, K. E., Hamlett, K. W., & Spock, A. (1992). Stress, coping, and family functioning in the psychological adjustment of mothers of children and adolescents with cystic fibrosis. *Journal of Pediatric Psychology, 17,* 573-585.

Turnbull, A. P., & Turnbull, H. R. (1986). *Families, Professional, and Exceptionality: A Special Partnership (3rd Ed.).* Upper Saddle, N.J.: Prentice Hall.

Wikler, L. (1986). Periodic stresses of families of older mentally retarded children: An exploratory study. *American Journal of Mental Deficiency, 90,* 703-706.

Wikler, L., Wasow, M., & Hatfield, E. (1981). Chronic sorrow revisited: Parents vs. professional depiction of the adjustment of parents of mentally retarded children. *American Journal of Orthopsychiatry, 51,* 63-70.

Wolf, L. C., Noh, S., Fisman, S. N., & Speechly, M. (1989). Brief report: Psychological effects of parenting stress on parents of autistic children. *Journal of Autism and Developmental Disorders, 19,* 157-166.

Emotional Availability is Predictive of the Emotional Aspects of Children's "School Readiness"

Zeynep Biringen, Shauna Skillern, Jen Mone
Dept. of Human Development & Family Studies
Colorado State University

Robert Pianta
University of Virginia

How a child fares socially and emotionally in the early years of school, particularly kindergarten, appears to have major consequences for the child's later adaptation to school and for a child's school trajectory (Alexander & Entwisle, 1988). In the present study, we focused on the links between a child's kindergarten adjustment and emotional availability in the mother-child relationship (assessed with the Emotional Availability Scales, EA; Biringen, Robinson, & Emde, 1998, 3rd edition), prior to kindergarten entry. EA includes 4 parental dimensions (sensitivity, structuring, nonintrusiveness, and nonhostility) and 2 child dimensions (responsiveness to parent and involvement of parent). Given so much emphasis on the construct of maternal sensitivity, we examined whether maternal sensitivity, assessed prior to school entry, predicts emotional aspects of children's "school readiness." In addition, we examined whether a larger emotional availability construct predicts additional variance in "school readiness" after controlling for sensitivity. Results indicated the value of moving beyond the maternal sensitivity construct in the prediction of children's adjustment to school.

This research was supported by NSF Grant # 9973396 awarded to the first author. We thank the study families for their dedicated participation in this research. Reprint requests should be sent to author Biringen: Dept. of Human Development & Family Studies, Colorado State University, Fort Collins, CO 80523.

Pathways to successful school adjustment are set early in the educational process. Evidence suggests that social and relational processes in the early years of school play a key role in establishing the foundation for a child's later adaptation to school and for the child's school trajectory (Alexander & Entwisle, 1988). In other words, the child who begins school in an interpersonally skilled and emotionally well-regulated manner is more likely to continue on this positive school trajectory than the child who enters school with a problematic relational profile. Clearly, the social and emotional adjustment is an aspect of a child's "school readiness" (Ladd & Price, 1989; Pianta & Walsh, 1996).

For many children, kindergarten marks the earliest point of formal schooling in the country. Thus, it is important to focus on the transition to kindergarten and the kindergarten year as the context for children's introduction to school and to begin to understand the factors forecasting kindergarten adjustment. If we can better understand the factors contributing to a successful social and emotional beginning for kindergarten children, we may be able to design interventions that best prepare children for the social challenges of being in school. As Ladd and Price (1987, p. 169) have noted, "the ability to forecast transition outcomes may enable investigators to design programs that facilitate children's competence or prevent subsequent maladaptation." For theoretical, intervention, and social policy reasons, then, it is particularly important to understand what predicts kindergarten adaptation (La Paro & Pianta, 2001; Pianta & McCoy, 1999).

Although kindergarten adjustment may be affected by numerous factors, the role of the family has emerged as a key predictor. For example, Isley, O'Neill, and Parke (1996) have found that the affective quality as well as appropriate control during parent-child interactions, and particularly affective quality, prior to school entry, predicted children's adjustment in kindergarten, as rated by classmates. Pianta, Smith, and Reeve (1991) found that observed mother-child interaction, prior to school entry (particularly maternal supportive presence, quality of instruction, child affection, task orientation, and self-esteem) predicted children's behavior problems and competence in kindergarten, as rated by teachers.

Inspired by attachment theory and research (Ainsworth, Blehar, Waters, & Wall, 1978), the importance of maternal sensitivity has also been examined. In attachment work, maternal sensitivity is seen as the mechanism by which a child gains a sense of security and trust in the mother-child relationship. In terms of the school setting, it is thought that when a mother is more sensitive, a child gains a sense of what secure and appropriately connected relationships are like, and goes into the school setting with the expectation as well as skills to initiate and maintain relationships with others, including peers and teachers (Sroufe & Fleeson, 1986).

Children whose mothers provided sensitive care (responsive and attuned to the child's behavioral cues and needs) during the preschool period were less likely to be judged by teachers as having internalizing or externalizing behavior problems. Maternal sensitivity during the infant, toddler, and preschool years emerged as a consistent predictor of children's social functioning in school, and seemed to predict better than even maternal depressive symptoms (NICHD Early Child Care Research Network, 2002, 2003). In a separate study, mothers' sensitive care of their behaviorally inhibited or wary children (a temperament characteristic) was associated with more optimal adjustment in kindergarten (Early et al., 2002); such a connection was not found for children who were not behaviorally inhibited. Thus a temperament characteristic that could mitigate a successful transition into a new environment appeared to have been modified by earlier sensitive care by the mother.

Although the sensitivity construct occupies a central place in attachment theory, in fact, a comprehensive meta-analysis has indicated that sensitivity explains only a modest portion of the variance in attachment (van Izjendoorn, 1995). Despite this important finding, most attachment research and research investigating the attachment-relevant contribution of mother-child interactions has focused predominantly on this construct, both before and after this meta-analysis.

We investigate links between family processes and kindergarten adjustment from the perspective of a larger construct "emotional availability". Mahler, Pine, and Bergman (1975) used this term to describe a supportive maternal presence, specifically in the context of the child's exploratory forays and practicing of autonomy. In their view, the mother's "quiet supportiveness" signals her encouragement and acceptance of such explorations and of the child's returns for emotional refueling. Emotional availability as described by Emde (1980) refers to an individual's emotional responsiveness and affective attunement to another's needs and goals; key is the individual's acceptance of a wide range of emotions rather than responsiveness solely to distressful situations. Emde and Easterbrooks (1985) stated that "emotional availability will therefore refer to the degree to which each partner expresses emotions and is responsive to the emotions of the other" (p. 80).

The assessment of emotional availability (EA) began with a 1991 paper by Biringen and Robinson (1991) in which they conceptualized separable dimensions of parental and child emotional qualities. Further refinements were described by Biringen (2000), such that EA now includes four qualities of parental emotional availability to the child (sensitivity, structuring, nonintrusiveness, nonhostility) and two aspects of child emotional availability to the parent (responsiveness to mother and the involvement of mother). Each aspect emphasizes the importance of the "emotional" qualities of an interaction, that is, whether the parent and child are free to emit appropriate emotional signals and to receive/interpret the emotional signals of the other.

Because the larger emotional availability construct includes not only the traditional maternal sensitivity construct researched heavily in the field of attachment, but also a number of other maternal qualities as well as an understanding of the child's perspective on the relationship, we will be able to examine whether the larger EA construct has predictive significance for children's adjustment to school. In addition to the well-known construct of caregiver sensitivity, EA construct includes caregiver structuring, nonintrusiveness, and nonhostility. On the child's side, EA includes child responsiveness to the caregiver and child involvement. Structuring refers to the appropriate level of suggestions and leads that support a child's explorations and play. Caregiver nonintrusiveness, on the other hand, refers to the extent to which the caregiver is appropriately available for interaction; an adult can be nonintrusive and passive/unstructuring or nonintrusive in an appropriately available way. Caregiver nonhostility refers to the ability of the adult to regulate emotions so that he or she does not need to control the child through anger; nonhostility is described in overt ways as well as the more covert forms. The child's side of emotional availability refers to the child's view of the relationship. Child responsiveness refers to the child's affective reactions to the caregiver and the child's eagerness to respond to the caregiver's bids. The child's involvement refers to the child's interest in including the caregiver in interaction.

This larger construct has been tested in numerous independent laboratories, with promising results. With very young infants, Kogan and Carter (1995) found that EA during free play was associated with "reunion" behavior after the still-face situation. Aviezar, Sagi, Joels, and Ziv (1999) tested three components of the attachment transmission model, using the Adult Attachment Interview (AAI), individual dimensions of emotional availability, and the strange situation classification, in kibbutz dyads, and found that secure attachment representations were related to EA, particularly maternal sensitivity, child responsiveness, and child involvement of mother. Biringen, Brown, Donaldson, Green, Krcmarik, and Lovas (2000) found relations between maternal adult attachment representations (using the AAI) and maternal and child emotional availability in a sample of prekindergartners. Moving to older children, Easterbrooks, Bieseker and Lyons-Ruth (2000) found that infant-mother attachment in the strange situation predicted each of the individual EA dimensions in free play as well as reunion contexts with the mother seven years later. Siri-Oyen, Landy, and Hillburn-Cobb (2000) found that maternal secure attachment (using the AAI) was related to EA in a sample of aggressive preschoolers.   Further, Pressman, Pipp-Siegel,

Yoshinaga-Itano, Kubicek, and Emde (2000) have examined the link between EA and indices of child development. They found that maternal as well as child EA in a group of mother-toddler pairs were predictive of the child's language gains two years later in a sample of deaf/hard-of-hearing toddlers.

We assessed emotional availability both in free play and reunion contexts because according to attachment theory stressful and nonstressful contexts are important to examine separately (Ainsworth, Blehar, Waters, & Wall, 1978). Emotional availability was expected to predict kindergarten adjustment, even after controlling for other potentially relevant qualities, such as the extent of pre-school experience and children's language ability. This longitudinal design, examining emotional availability of mother to child and of the child to the mother prior to school entry and child adjustment soon after the transition into kindergarten as well as at the end of the kindergarten year, enabled us to understand the role of EA at a time when the child is faced with a series of new challenges.

We assessed children's kindergarten relationships and adjustment through a multi-method approach—via objective observations, teacher reports, and child interviews. Although a number of studies on this topic have utilized teacher reports, to our knowledge no prior studies on family-kindergarten links have used objective observations and obtained the child's perspective on relationships. Child qualities, such as aggression and victimization at school were observed in the classrooms, with observations being conducted soon after the kindergarten transition as well as at the end of the school year. Teachers also reported on children's adjustment with peers and with teachers, at the end of the fall semester and then again at the end of the school year. In addition, at the end of the school year, children were interviewed about their loneliness at school. We hypothesized that the larger emotional availability construct would predict child outcomes better than the maternal sensitivity construct.

Method

Participants

The participants consisted of 57 mother-child pairs. The sample was diverse in terms of educational level and occupational status of the families. The educational level of the mothers ranged from those who completed middle school to those who completed masters degrees. There were 26 boys and 31 girls in the sample; all children were 4 years of age at the prekindergarten phase. No children who waited an extra year to enter kindergarten were enrolled in the study. Most of the sample was Caucasian (39 mothers responded to this optional question), with one Asian, and one African-American in the sample.

Procedure

The procedure for the study involved data collection during the spring/summer months before kindergarten entry (prekindergarten phase) as well as during the kindergarten year (kindergarten phase). Parents were approached during registration for kindergarten at two elementary schools serving the most socioeconomically diverse populations in a small college town in Colorado. They were told about the Transition to Elementary School Project (a study to examine family/child factors affecting successful adjustment to kindergarten) and asked for their names and phone numbers for future contact. All parents coming in for kindergarten registration were interested in giving us their phone numbers for future contact. When contacted by phone, over 80% of mothers consented to participate.

The prekindergarten phase was conducted in our laboratory at Colorado State University. After the research assistant explained the study in detail and obtained informed consent, mothers and children were asked to sit at a table and play with an Etch-A-Sketch. Instructions were for the mother to operate the vertical dial and for the child to operate the horizontal dial to create first a house and second a boat; sketched (house and boat) models on paper were placed in front of the mother-child dyad; the episode lasted 5-6 minutes. Following the Etch-A-Sketch play, the research assistant replaced the Etch-A-Sketch with Playmobile toys (knights and princesses). Instructions to the mother-child dyad were that they should "play as they normally would with these toys". At the end of 15 minutes, the assistant returned and asked the child to help clean up the toys. This set of interactions was videotaped with a single camera on a tripod; the observational EA Scales were used to evaluate the 20 minutes of videotaped mother-child play.

Mothers and children were then separated, with mothers going to a room down the hall to complete other assessments and the child remaining in the laboratory for the language assessment—the Expressive One-Word Vocabulary Test (EOWVT; Brownell, 2000). After the separation (which lasted approximately 90 minutes), the mother-child dyad was then reunited and the "reunion" lasted 5 minutes. No instructions were given for the reunion. The EA Scales were again used to evaluate the 5-minute reunion.

During the kindergarten phase, target children were observed in their kindergarten classrooms; such observations were conducted *in vivo*. They were observed for two or more half-days (mornings or afternoons, depending on when the target child was attending kindergarten) during the first semester of the kindergarten year (Time 1) and two or more days during the second semester of kindergarten (Time 2). The observation protocol was as follows: Target child is observed for 3 seconds, followed by enough time to mark a tally. Each child was observed for a total of 540 tallies. Inter-rater reliabilities were done by having two raters simultaneously engaging in the observation protocol. The two observers remained in synchrony by signaling each other at the end of the 3 seconds of observation.

At the end of each semester (Time 1 and Time 2), the kindergarten teachers were given a packet of questionnaires for each target child. The packet consisted of the Teacher-Child Rating Scale and the Student-Teacher Relationship Scale.

At the end of the kindergarten year, in the home or lab, based on family choice, children were orally interviewed using the Loneliness and Social Dissatisfaction Questionnaire, adapted for kindergarten children (Cassidy & Asher, 1992).

Measures

Emotional Availability. Observed mother-child interactions were coded using the 3rd ed. of the Emotional Availability Scales (EA; Biringen et al., 1998), including 4 maternal scales (sensitivity, structuring, nonintrusiveness, and non-hostility) and 2 child scales (responsiveness to mother and involvement of mother). Sensitivity is a 9-point scale; other dimensions of maternal EA are 5-point scales. The child EA dimensions are 7-point scales. These observational scales are intercorrelated at moderate to high levels. EA has been used in numerous studies, both nationally and internationally (Aviezar et al., 1999; Easterbrooks & Biringen, 2000; Easterbrooks et al., 2000). Each of the parent-child interaction contexts (reunion and play) were scored separately for EA. Cohen's kappas between two raters ranged between .82 and .85 on 10 cases. One of the raters, blind to all information about the project, then went on to score all other cases; the single rater's scores rather than the conferenced scores were used in all cases. Emotional availability score is the sum of all of the 6 scales. For analyses, we did not include the sensitivity measure and refer to the composite as the emotional availability subcomposite or EA subcomposite.

Child Observations. Child Aggression and Victimization were observed. Aggression referred to the child expressing anger or rough behavior to another child; this measure included both verbal and physical indices of aggression. Victimization referred to the child being the recipient of another's aggression; this measure could also be verbal or physical indices of aggression. Using these two dimensions, the target child was observed in three different situations: recess, semi-structured activities (in which the child had an activity to complete but was not being instructed by the teacher), and structured activities (in which the teacher was providing instruction).

Teacher report of classroom behavior. The Teacher-Child Rating Scale (TCRS), a 38-item questionnaire was developed by Hightower et al. (1986). The individual items load on seven factor-based subscales: conduct problems, learning problems, shy/anxious problems, frustration tolerance, work habits, assertive social skills and peer sociability. Based on intercorrelations and conceptual similarity, the TCRS was aggregated by combining peer social skills, task orientation, assertiveness, and frustration tolerance to form a Positive Skills composite. The Acting Out and Shy/Anxious subscales were aggregated to form a Problematic Adjustment composite. (In our work, we have used both the TCRS and the Achenbach and Edelbrock, 1986, Child Behavior Checklist, with greater variability in teachers' responses on the TCRS in unselected samples.) Cronbach's alphas were high (average above .90); the TCRS correlates significantly and highly with other meaningful school-based indices, such as grades.

Student-Teacher Relationship Scale (STRS). This measure is used to determine whether the teacher views his/her relationship with the target child as positive or negative. A child's relationship with the teacher has been linked to school adjustment and the child's behavior in the home. Because prior work has indicated the usefulness of the Conflict measure, which addresses the degree to which the child and teacher get angry with each other (Pianta, personal communication, 2002), we focused on this aspect of the teacher-child relationship. The Cronbach's alphas for Conflict was .92 (Pianta, 1994).

Loneliness and Social Dissatisfaction Questionnaire. This measure provides an assessment of a child's overall feelings of Loneliness in a school setting. The questions in the measure concern feelings of inadequacy in a social setting, loneliness, self-perceptions of peer status, and an assessment of whether a child's relationship needs are being met. In an attempt to make the child more comfortable with the questions being asked, filler questions were included that focused on the child's likes and favorite activities. Children were shown 3 faces, one smiling, one neutral, and the other frowning, and asked to point to the picture that showed how they typically feel in the described situation. To familiarize the children with the procedure, they were asked how much they liked ice cream and all children pointed to the smiling face. The child's score on Loneliness could range from 16 to 46, with a high score indicating more Loneliness. A factor analysis of the measure showed that the main items, excluding the filler questions, loaded about .30. Internal consistency was determined using Cronbach's alpha and found to be .79. The most Loneliness was reported by kindergarten children classified as insecure/resistant in the strange situation procedure during infancy, the least by the children who were classified as insecure/avoidant, and an intermediate level was reported by those classified as secure during infancy (Cassidy & Asher, 1992).

Language assessments. To assess a child's expressive language competence, the Expressive One-Word Picture Vocabulary Test (EOWPVT) was used. The EOWPVT measures a child's ability to name illustrated actions or concepts. It is designed to measure the child's speaking vocabulary. The child is shown a series of illustrations depicting an action, object, or concept, and asked to name each illustration. Cronbach's alphas for this measure ranged from .93 to .98, and split-half coefficients ranged from .96 to .99. Expressive language competence was shown to be highly correlated with other vocabulary tests such as the WISC-III (Brownell, 2000).

Results

First, to determine if there were significant correlations between background variables (gender of child, age of child, amount of preschool experience, expressive language competence, and mother's education) and child outcomes, zero-order correlations were computed. Expressive language competence and amount of preschool experience were correlated with some, but not all, of the outcome measures. For uniformity in the plan of analyses, we entered these two background measures at the first step in Hierarchical Multiple Regression (HMR) Analyses, shown in the tables. At the second step, we entered maternal sensitivity and at the third step, we entered the EA subcomposite, which is the sum of all EA dimensions that did not include maternal sensitivity. For these analyses, the scores for EA play and EA reunion were aggregated to yield robust EA composites; patterns of relations were similar for play (vs. reunion) and the study variables. The information obtained from Time 1 and Time 2 were analyzed separately since the patterns of intercorrelations were actually quite different, as for example, Aggression and Victimization being unrelated to EA at Time 1 but being related at Time 2. Discrete counts of aggression and victimization were first normalized before being subjected to statistical analyses. Degrees of freedom for step one are 2, 39, for step 2 they are 1, 38 and for step 3 they are 1, 37.

EA and Child Observations

Amount of preschool experience and language competence did not significantly predict child aggression in kindergarten at Time 1 or Time 2. The EA subcomposite which did not include maternal sensitivity, explained 15% of the *additional* variance in aggression at Time 2, even after controlling for the background variables and maternal sensitivity, suggesting that the EA dimensions besides sensitivity are helpful in predicting children's adjustment in kindergarten. See Table 1.

Table 1 Relations between EA and observations of the children in kindergarten

	Aggression Time 1			Aggression Time 2		
	β	ΔR^2	ΔF	β	ΔR^2	ΔF
Step 1						
Preschool Experience	-.16			.00		
Language	.06	.03	.51	-.05	.01	.36
Step 2						
Sensitivity	-.23	.04	1.61	-.30	.07	2.76
Step 3						
EA subcomp.	-.46	.05	2.17	-.77	.15	6.97**

Note: ΔR^2 = Change at each step in the Multiple R^2; ΔF = Change at each step in the F value. EAsubcomp. = EA subcomposite or the sum of the EA dimensions that does not include sensitivity.
* p < .05; **p < .01.

Table 2: Relations between EA and observations of the children's victimization in kindergarten

	Victimization Time 1			Victimization Time 2		
	β	ΔR^2	ΔF	β	ΔR^2	ΔF
Step 1						
Preschool Experience	.06			.06		
Language	.05	.01	.16	.05	.01	.16
Step 2:						
Sensitivity	-.30	.07	2.67	-.30	.07	2.67
Step 3						
EA subcomp	-.76	.14	6.6**	-.76	.14	6.63**

Note: ΔR^2 = Change at each step in the Multiple R^2; ΔF = Change at each step in the F value. EAsubcomp. = EA subcomposite or the sum of the EA dimensions that does not include sensitivity.
* p < .05; **p < .01.

We next examined Victimization in the kindergarten classroom. At Time 1 as well as Time 2, Victimization is predicted by the EA subcomposite, contributing an additional and significant 14% of the variance, after controlling for the background variables as well as maternal sensitivity. These findings suggest once again that EA dimensions other than maternal sensitivity play an important role in prediction of children's adjustment in kindergarten. See Table 2.

EA and Teachers' Reports

TCRS. At Time 1, The step 1 background variables predicted Positive Social Skills, but EA sensitivity did not contribute additional significant variance. However, at Time 2, the EA subcomposite added an additional and significant 9% of the variance, which was significant, again indicating that the EA dimensions other than sensitivity explain the variance in Positive Social Skills. See Table 3.

Table 3: Relations between EA and teacher-reported positive social skills in kindergarten

	Positive Skills Time 1			Positive Skills Time 2		
	β	ΔR^2	ΔF	β	ΔR^2	ΔF
Step 1						
Preschool Experience	-.18				.08	
Language	.61	.36	10.64***	.45	.23	5.56**
Step 2						
Sensitivity	.18	.02	1.35	.08	.00	.21
Step 3						
EA subcomp.	.34	.03	1.79	.58	.09	4.59*

Note: ΔR^2 = Change at each step in the Multiple R^2; ΔF = Change at each step in the F value. EAsubcomp. = EA subcomposite or the sum of the EA dimensions that does not include sensitivity.
* p < .05; **p < .01; ***p <.001.

Problem Behaviors. At Time 1, step 1 variables were significant and maternal sensitivity contributed an additional and significant 10% of the variance in explaining Problem Behaviors, and the EA subcomposite explained an additional significant 12% of the variance. At Time 2, only the EA ubcomposite contributed significant variance to explaining Problem Behaviors (a full and significant 15%), even after controlling for the background variables as well as maternal sensitivity in prior steps of the analyses. See Table 4.

Table 4: Relations between EA and teacher-reported problem behaviors in kindergarten

	Problem Behaviors Time 1			Problem Behaviors Time 2		
	β	ΔR^2	ΔF	β	ΔR^2	ΔF
Step 1						
Preschool Experience	.24				.07	
Language	-.39	.17	3.96*	-.27	.07	1.52
Step 2						
Sensitivity	-.38	.10	5.33*	-.17	.02	.84
Step 3						
EA subcomp.	-.68	.12	6.97**	-.76	.15	7.09**

Note: ΔR^2 = Change at each step in the Multiple R^2; ΔF = Change at each step in the F value. EAsubcomp. = EA subcomposite or the sum of the EA dimensions that does not include sensitivity.
* p < .05; **p < .01.

STRS. The Conflict Scale was used, and at Time 2, the EA subcomposite explained a significant 10% of the variance, even after controlling for the background variables and maternal sensitivity. See Table 5.

EA and Child Interviews About Loneliness

Children's Loneliness was assessed only at the end of the kindergarten year and was predicted only by the EA subcomposite (explaining an additional and significant 17% of the variance), even after controlling for other variables. See Table 6.

Table 5: Relations between EA and teacher-reported conflict in kindergarten

	Conflict Time 1			Conflict Time 2		
	β	ΔR^2	ΔF	β	ΔR^2	ΔF
Step 1						
Preschool Experience	.30			.18		
Language	-.29	.14	3.06+	-.20	.06	1.18
Step 2						
Sensitivity	-.29	.06	2.86+	-.10	.01	.29
Step 3						
EA subcomp.	-.32	.03	1.24	-.62	.10	4.24*

Note: ΔR^2 = Change at each step in the Multiple R^2; ΔF = Change at each step in the F value. EAsubcomp. = EA subcomposite or the sum of the EA dimensions that does not include sensitivity.
* $p < .05$; ** $p < .01$.

Table 6: Emotional Availability and Children's Loneliness

	β	ΔR^2	ΔF
Step 1			
Preschool Experience	.23		
Language	-.24	.09	1.93
Step 2			
Sensitivity	.01	.00	.00
Step 3			
EA subcomp.	-.85	.17	8.81**

Note: ΔR^2 = Change at each step in the Multiple R^2; ΔF = Change at each step in the F value. EAsubcomp. = EA subcomposite or the sum of the EA dimensions that does not include sensitivity.
* $p < .05$; ** $p < .01$.

Discussion

The findings of this study indicate that emotional availability in the mother-child relationship is an important attachment-relevant concept to use in school research. Although maternal sensitivity by itself was only a modest predictor of child outcomes in this study, the larger EA construct was useful as a predictive tool, even after controlling for sensitivity.

Although sensitivity is a well-known attachment construct, it appears that other maternal and child qualities described by the larger EA construct also are important in preparing children for the world of school. A quality such as maternal structuring may teach a child to display appropriate behaviors in school settings, as for example, free play, semi-structured activities, and structured activities. Maternal nonintrusiveness might help a child to have enough space and opportunity to display assertive social skills. Maternal nonhostility may help a child to regulate her or his own emotions in a nonangry and well-regulated manner. Further, a child's emotional responsiveness and interest in involving the mother in interaction may create a template for emotionally available relationships with peers as well as with the teacher. The sensitivity construct simply does not predict as well as the larger EA umbrella.

The present study is the first to examine the links between maternal emotional qualities and a child's social adjustment at school by using a longitudinal, multi-method approach, using teacher reports, direct observations, and child interviews. EA prior to school entry was predictive of children's kindergarten adjustment, including observed aggression, observed victimization, teacher-reported positive social skills, problematic adjustment, conflict with the teacher, as well as child-reported loneliness at school.

It appears that these additional EA dimensions are important not only for kindergarten children's adjustment, as was uncovered in the present investigation, but also in predicting infant-parent attachment security (Biringen, Damon, Grigg, Mone, Pipp-Siegel, & Skillern, in press). However, given that all of the EA dimensions were scored by the same coder and likely because of this interrelated, we were not in a position to assess whether the EA dimensions could predict differential aspects of kindergarten adjustment.

The findings further indicate that a substantial number of families (approximately 25% of mother-child pairs) experience emotional availability that is at or below the median (e.g., < 5 in one or more aspects of emotional availability) for this unselected, volunteer sample. Many of these mothers likely had few clues that anything was remiss in the mother-child relationship. Given the relation between emotional availability and children's school adjustment, it behooves families to question and, if needed, improve the emotional availability in parent-child relationships. Emotional availability assessment may therefore be a powerful tool in understanding a child's emotional adjustment, and hence his or her adjustment potential in a variety of contexts, including the context of kindergarten.

References

Achenbach, T. M., & Edelbrock, C. S. (1983). *Manual for the Child Behavior Checklist and Revised Child Behavior Profile.* Burlington, VT: University of Vermont. Department of Psychiatry.

Ainsworth, M. D. S., Blehar, M. C., Waters, E. E., & Wall, S. (1978). *Patterns of attachment: A psychological study of the strange situation.* Hillsdale, NJ: Lawrence Erlbaum.

Alexander, K.L., & Entwisle, D.R. (1988). Achievement in the first 2 years of school: Patterns and processes. *Monographs of the Society for Research in Child Development, 53,* 1-157.

Aviezar, O., Sagi, A., Joels, T., & Ziv, Y. (1999). Emotional availability and attachment representations in kibbutz infants and their mothers. *Developmental Psychology, 35(3),* 811-821.

Biringen, Z. (2000). Emotional availability: Conceptualization and research findings. *American Journal of Orthopsychiatry, 70,* 104-114.

Biringen, Z., Brown, D., Donaldson, L., Green, S., Krcmarik, S., & Lovas, G. (2000). Adult Attachment Interview: Linkages with dimensions of the emotional availability and their pre-kindergarteners. *Attachment and Human Development, 2,* (No. 2), 188-202.

Biringen, Z., Damon, J., Grigg, W., Mone, J., Pipp-Siegel, S., & Skillern, S. (in press). Differential predictions of attachment security from emotional availability. *Infant Mental Health Journal.*

Biringen, Z., & Robinson, J. (1991). Emotional availability: A reconceptualization for research. *American Journal of Orthopsychiatry, 61,* 258-271.

Biringen, Z., Robinson, J., & Emde, R.N. (1998). *The emotional availability scales* (3rd ed.), unpublished manuscript, Department of Human Development & Family Studies, Colorado State University, Fort Collins, CO.

Brownell, R. (2000). *Expressive One-Word Picture Vocabulary Test Manual.* Academic Therapy Publications: Novato, California.

Brownell, R. (2000). *Receptive One-Word Picture Vocabulary Test Manual.* Academic Therapy Publications: Novato, California.

Cassidy, J., & Asher, S. R. (1992). Loneliness and peer relations in young children. *Child Development, 63,* 350-365.

Early, D.M., Rimm-Kaufman, S.E., Cox, M. J., Saluja, G., Pianta, R. C., Bradley, R.H., & Payne, C. C. (2002). Maternal sensitivity and child wariness in the transition to kindergarten. *Parenting: Science and Practice, 2,* 355-377.

Easterbrooks, M. A., & Biringen, Z. (2000). Guest editors' introduction to the special issue: Mapping the terrain of emotional availability and attachment. *Attachment and Human Development, 2,* 123-129.

Easterbrooks, M. A., Biesecker, G., & Lyons-Ruth, K. (2000). Infancy predictors of emotional availability in middle childhood: The roles of attachment security and maternal depressive symptomatology. *Attachment and Human Development, 2* (2), 123-129.

Emde, R. N. (1980). Emotional availability: A reciprocal reward system for infants and parents with implications for prevention of psychosocial disorders. In P.M. Taylor (Ed.), *Parent-infant relationships.* Orlando, FL: Grune & Stratton.

Emde, R. N., & Easterbrooks, M. A. (1985). Assessing emotional availability in early development. In D.K. Frankenberg, R.N. Emde, & J.W. Sullivan (Eds.), *Early identification of children at risk: An international perspective* (pp. 79-101). New York: Plenum Press.

Hightower, A. D., Work, W. C., Cowen, E. L., Lotyezewski, B. S., Spinell, A. P., Guare, J. C., & Rohrbeck, C. A. (1986). The Teacher-Child Rating Scale: A brief objective measure of elementary children's school problem behaviors and competencies. *School Psychology Review, 15,* 393-409.

Isley, S., O'Neill, R., & Parke, R. D. (1996). The relation of parental affect and control behaviors to children's classroom acceptance: A concurrent and predictive analysis. *Early Education and Development, 7,* 7-23.

Kogan, N., & Carter, A. S. (1996). Mother-infant reengagement following the still-face: The role of maternal emotional availability in infant affect regulation. *Infant Behavior and Development, 19,* 359-370.

Ladd, G. W., & Price, J. M. (1987). Predicting children's social and school adjustment following the transition from preschool to kindergarten. *Child Development, 58,* 1168-1189.

La Paro, K. M., & Pianta, R. C. (2001). Predicting children's competence in the early school years: A meta-analytic review. *Review of Educational Research, 70,* 443-484.

Mahler, M. S., Pine, F., & Bergman, A. (1975). *The psychological birth of the human infant: Symbiosis and individuation.* New York: Basic Books.

NICHD Early Child Care Research Network. (2002). Early child care and children's development prior to school entry. *American Educational Research Journal, 39,* 133-164.

NICHD Early Child Care Research Network. (2003). Social functioning in first grade: Associations with earlier home and child care predictors and with current classroom experiences. *Child Development, 74(6),* 1639-1662.

Pianta, R. C. (1994). Patterns of relationships between children and kindergarten teachers. *Journal of School Psychology, 32,* 15-32.

Pianta, R. C., & McCoy, S. J. (1999). The first day of school: The predictive validity of early school screening. *Journal of Applied Developmental Psychology, 18,* 1-22.

Pianta, R. C., Smith, N., & Reeve, R. E. (1991). Observing mother and child behavior in a problem-solving situation at school entry: Relations with classroom adjustment, *School Psychology Quarterly, 6,* 1-15.

Pianta, R. C., & Walsh, D. J. (1996). *High-risk children in schools: Constructing sustaining relationships.* New York: Routledge.

Pressman, L. J., Pipp-Siegel, S., Yoshinaga-Itano, C., Kubicek, L. F., & Emde, R. N. (April, 1998). The relation of hearing status and emotional availability to child language gain. *Volta Review.*

Siri-Oyen, A., Landy, S., & Hilburn-Cobb, C. (2000). Maternal attachment and sensitivity in an at-risk sample. *Attachment and Human Development, 2(2),* 203-217.

Sroufe, L. A., & Fleeson, J. Attachment and the construction of relationships. In W. Hartup & Z. Rubin (Eds.) *The nature and development of relationships.* Hillsdale, NJ: Erlbaum.

van Ijzendoorn, M. H. (1995). Adult attachment representations, parental responsiveness, and infant attachment: A meta-analysis on the predictive validity of the Adult Attachment Interview. *Psychological Bulletin, 117,* 387-403.

Dynamic Assessment with Young Children: We've Come a Long Way Baby!

Carol S. Lidz

This article reviews the current status of the use of dynamic assessment with children of preschool age. The dynamic assessment model is briefly described, with specific procedures and issues of using this approach with young children discussed. The author concludes that dynamic assessment offers a viable approach for use by psychologists in early childhood settings, though further development remains to be accomplished.

In 1983 I first discussed the relevance of dynamic assessment (DA) for preschool children. At that time, the primary models had not yet been applied with individuals of this age, and specific procedures that were even remotely dynamic and appropriate for this population were difficult to find. More than twenty years later, the scene has changed. The primary models have not only expanded and developed, but considerable research has been accomplished (www.dynamicassessment.com); most relevantly, procedures for use with very young and not so very young children are now increasingly available. We have indeed come a long way. In this article, I review the dynamic assessment procedures for use with young children that are currently available. I also discuss some related issues and offer commentary regarding the implications of this model for early childhood psychologists.

What is Dynamic Assessment?

Dynamic assessment is a generic term for a variety of procedures that most consistently share the characteristics of following a test-intervene-retest administration and embedding interaction with the child within the assessment. The

Carol S. Lidz, Psy.D., retired, 2206 Lombard Street, Philadelphia, PA 19146.
email: zdilsc@aol.com

purpose of this interaction is to promote a higher level of functioning of the child and to allow assessors to draw conclusions about the qualities or content of the interaction that promote this change. Dynamic assessment tends to focus on the process and processes of learning rather than on its final products, although levels of performance within specific content domains may be addressed and incorporated. Both content and degree of structure vary considerably from procedure to procedure, depending upon the theoretical model as well as the proposed use of the approach. For example, there are approaches that are designed as alternatives to traditional tests of intelligence that use generic reasoning tasks; there are approaches that focus on specific processes such as memory, and there are those that incorporate academic content such as reading or mathematics. Therefore, the term "dynamic assessment" applies more to how the assessment is conducted (with embedded intervention) than to what is assessed.

Because the intervention portion of most dynamic approaches to assessment tends to address the executive processes of the learner, there has been considerably more attention to development of procedures for older learners. Interventions often incorporate principles and strategies for task solution that are beyond the capabilities of what would be expected for very young children. However, the neuropsychological development of young children is not devoid of executive processing, and it is during preschool years, even early preschool years, that metacognitive capacities in fact rapidly emerge. The degree of variability of this emergence during these early years may in fact provide the basis for some very relevant information that can be uniquely tapped by dynamic procedures as a means of informing intervention (e.g., Luria, 1979; Siegler, 1983).

The attraction to dynamic assessment rests primarily in its ability to link assessment with intervention as well as in its appropriateness for individuals from culturally and linguistically diverse backgrounds (Lidz, 2001; Lidz & Macrine, 2001; Peña, 2000). The work of Banks and Neisworth (1995) with Indian families (see also Robinson-Zañartu [1996] and Peña [2000]) with Latino populations is particularly important for the latter.

What we know now about this model is first, that it is often possible to promote significant positive change in the levels of children's performance in response to the interventions offered during the course of the assessment. Second, the correlations between pretests and posttests, though significant, are far from perfect, and rank orders may in fact differ dramatically following exposure of children to the brief embedded interventions. This suggests that diagnostic conclusions based on traditional approaches, equivalent to the pretest phase of the dynamic model, may be spurious. Third, the post-intervention results are often better predictors of achievement than the pretest, or more static/traditional, results (Guthke & Wingenfeld, 1992; Lidz & Greenberg, 1997; Lidz, Jepsen, & Miller, 1997; Sternberg et al., 2002; Tzuriel, 2001). Finally, the information offered, such as the child's responsiveness to intervention, is simply not available from other approaches, since the dynamic model is defined by its inclusion of intervention, differentiating it from other approaches.

To illustrate how I have used the dynamic model within the larger assessment process, I will summarize a case that appears in greater detail in Lidz (2003).

> This is the case of Peter, who was referred prior to his entry to kindergarten. His school system had already carried out psychological and educational assessments, but his parents wished for an independent evaluation regarding the question of what services he would need. Peter was a five year old who was adopted from an East European orphanage at the age of three years, where he resided since the age of 18 months. There was no early history except that the orphanage environment was considered relatively benign. He had been retained for an additional year in his preschool where his teacher recommended a psychological assessment because of his lack of progress, his high activity level and sensory integration issues. He was diagnosed Attention Deficit Hyperactivity Disorder (ADHD) and on medication; he had also been involved in short term sensory motor therapy. I did not wish to repeat what had been done by the school district's psychologist, so selected procedures that would explore the specific issues of concern, as well as those that emerged during the course of the assessment; these mainly concerned language. He was observed in play interaction with his mother. Some standardized procedures were administered to survey his skills with particular emphasis on language and visual-motor functions. Rating scales were completed by his parents related to his behavior at home as well as specific issues of attention. Informal procedures addressed phonological awareness, neuropsychological screening, and dynamic assessment of classification and story retelling selection from the author's Application of Cognitive Functions Scale (ACFS) procedure described below. The classification task showed that he had some emergent ability to make groups prior to intervention, but tended to use the blocks aggressively. With adult guidance, he was easily refocused. Following intervention that showed him strategies for forming and re-forming groups with blocks, he was able to apply the information introduced and able to function at a higher independent level. He also showed some, but limited, flexibility with re-grouping. With story retelling, he retained very little of the short story read to him prior to intervention, mentioning only one of the several characters and only the central action. Following intervention, he accurately recalled all of

the characters, presented information in the correct sequence, and repeated the central action. Peter profited a great deal from his active involvement in the interventions with which he was able to engage, and which successfully captured his attention. With his attention focused through this active involvement, he was able to profit from the instruction. The assessment found that he had most of the knowledge base for kindergarten but had ongoing needs for close supervision and individualized programming. He was a responsive learner with difficulty with self-regulation. He had significant differences between his higher level of functioning on spatial compared with lower level of functioning on language tasks. Peter's language foundation was in a language other than English. Special services of speech/language, occupational therapy, and small class placement were recommended. Specific instructional recommendations included pairing language with spatial-construction tasks, using the model-building intervention from the dynamic assessment to help with his narratives, involvement in stop and go activities and games to address issues of self-regulation, and assigning him a teaching role with other students to utilize his higher level skills in math, promote his self-confidence, and address self-regulation.

Dynamic assessment in Peter's case was very helpful in revealing his ability to profit from instruction under close supervision from an adult and active involvement in visual-spatial types of tasks to capture his attention and thereby promote his learning. In these circumstances, the lack of progress observed by his preschool teacher was turned around. Dynamic assessment also helped to suggest the potential usefulness of pairing verbal and spatial-constructive functions to address Peter's struggle with language. As is often the case with children from culturally different backgrounds, his mastery of English was not as deep as appeared from casual interactions with him, and it remained to be seen whether he had a language-based learning disorder or was struggling with English as a foreign language. English was his dominant language, and he was not at all functioning in the language to which he was first exposed, but, nevertheless, his exposure during his first critical three years was in this language environment.

Why Should Early Childhood Psychologists Be Interested?

There are two current "buzz" phrases that should suffice to justify the interest in dynamic assessment of psychologists working with any children, and, particularly, with young children. These are "responsiveness to intervention" and "evidence-based practice" (Gresham, 2004). These two concepts are now incorporated into mandates and standards applying to all children with special needs. The ability to address these two ideas has become basic to professional practice and job retention. Exactly what either of these means has yet to be adequately detailed, and it remains to be seen how these will play out in practice. As usual, good intent is balanced by the possibilities for abuse and misunderstanding. The intent of improving programming for children with special needs can easily be overtaken by administrative needs to reduce budgets by cutting services.

Dynamic assessment has much to offer that addresses both of these issues. First, the DA model by definition and design offers information regarding response to intervention. This is at the core of the model. Each DA session provides a mini-laboratory experiment that directly examines how and how well the child responds to the interventions embedded within the procedure, either by prescription or exploration. By the same token, the child's responsiveness provides the evidence on which to base instructional design. This should, of course, be followed up and monitored to document further how the child responds to the implementation of this evidence within the classroom setting. Evidence from studies of groups of children is becoming increasingly available (see website cited above), but it is the evidence that derives directly from the work with the individual child that has the most value and importance for designing the individual educational program.

What Is Currently Available?

The earliest work with young children that could be viewed as dynamic assessment was done by Haeussermann (1958). She worked primarily with children with cerebral palsy, and developed an informal, though well-elaborated, approach that followed errors or failures with a series of probes to explore the level at which the children could respond. This was subsequently developed into a more formalized procedure by Jedrysek, Klapper, Pope, and Wortis (1972). Although this approach can no longer be considered "currently available," (though Haeussermann's book can certainly be found), it is of historical importance, as Haeussermann can be considered the mother of dynamic assessment of young children.

Other historically relevant work that can still be found in the literature has been done by Burns, Vye, Bransford, Delclos, and Ogan (1987) as well as by Lidz and Thomas (1987). Burns et al. (1987) developed a Stencil Design Test that added seven designs to the original Grace Arthur Stencil Design Test, and simplified this original test so that only two stencils were necessary to create each design (one solid and one cut out). They also designed an Animal Stencil Test of 18 cards, consisting of 6 solid colors and 12 cut-outs. Intervention involved familiarization of the child with the cards and relevant attributes, teaching the child the rule for combining the stencils, and provision of elaborated feedback about the correctness of the child's performance.

Lidz and Thomas' (1987) Preschool Learning Assessment Device (PLAD) used two subtests from the Kaufman Assessment Battery for Children (Kaufman & Kaufman, 1983) as pre/post tests: Triangles and Matrices. These subtests were administered according to the standardized directions of the manual for both pretest and posttest. The intervention phase was designed to reflect Feuerstein's conceptualization of Mediated Learning Experience (e.g., Feuerstein, Rand, & Hoffman, 1979) that targeted the task analyses of these subtests provided in the K-ABC Interpretive Manual. The PLAD was administered to 60 Head Start children between the ages of three through five who had been referred for assessment regarding possible special needs by their regular classroom teachers. They were randomly assigned to one of two groups, an Experimental group that received mediated intervention between the pretest and posttest, and a Control group that received no mediation during this time (they were exposed to the materials and encouraged to play with them for a similar period of time, unfacilitated by the assessor). Two additional K-ABC subtests were administered as transfer tasks, and the teachers completed a social competency rating scale for predictive validity. The Experimental group obtained significantly higher gain scores than Controls on both the Triangles and Matrices subtests, with the Controls essentially showing no gains on either subtest. The Experimental group's scores on the Triangles subtest showed a stronger correlation with social competence than the Control's (.55 compared to .35), with no meaningful difference for the Matrices. There were no differences between groups on the transfer tasks. Reinharth (1989) had similar results with her thirty children with significant developmental delays. Reinharth found highly significant differences favoring the Experimental (mediated) over Control (unmediated) group. Unique to this study was the retesting of the participants two weeks following administration of the posttests. This yielded a further increase in the difference between the groups, with only the Experimental group showing continued gains.

Following this initial foray into development of a dynamic assessment procedure appropriate for use with young children, Lidz moved to Curriculum-Based Dynamic Assessment (CBDA; Lidz, 1991, 2003) to bring the approach closer to academic content and instruction. CBDA is a generic, overarching procedure that can be applied to virtually any content. The essence is to analyze both task and learner in relation to the basic mental processes reflected in task demands (viz. attention, perception, memory, language, cognition, and metacognition), to consider the nature and degree of match between the two (viz, what the task demands and what the learner brings), and to design interventions in terms of best instructional practices that address the primary processing demands that the learner needs to develop to achieve competence on the task. This approach was introduced by Lidz in 1991 and further elaborated and updated by Lidz in 2003. There is no age restriction, and CBDA is totally appropriate for use with very young children. However, it can be somewhat demanding for the assessor because of the need to custom-design interventions that relate to the specific content and processes related to that content. Jitendra, Rohena-Diaz, and Nolet (1998) demonstrated the usefulness of this CBDA model with children with language impairments. Further applications of dynamic assessment to academic content relevant to young children has been carried out by investigators such as Spector (1992), who focuses on phonemic awareness.

In an attempt to provide a more standardized "package" that could serve the multiple purposes of introducing assessors to dynamic assessment, providing data for research, and serving as a diagnostic screening tool for young children, Lidz, in collaboration with Jepsen (Lidz, 2000), developed the ACFS. The ACFS is curriculum-based in its incorporation of content that is typically included in most American preschool curricula; the six tasks tap the processes of classification, auditory and visual memory, pattern sequencing, planning, and perspective taking. Each task is administered in pretest-intervention-posttest format. The pretests and posttests have standardized instructions, and the interventions are prescribed and semi-scripted, designed to reflect current instructional best practices that communicate basic principles and strategies relevant for solving the specific tasks to which they are attached. The ACFS includes a Behavior Rating Scale, used to rate the degree of occurrence of seven characteristics observable during the pretest and mediation phases of task administration (namely, self-regulation, flexibility, perseverance, frustration tolerance, motivation, interactivity, and responsivity). The procedure is appropriate for individuals functioning within the three through five year age range. To date, at least twelve studies have been completed that address issues of reliability and validity, and it has been translated into Dutch, Romanian, and Spanish, as well as applied with children from England and Australia. The full administrative and technical manuals will be available in a forthcoming publication by Haywood and Lidz (in preparation).

Tzuriel (2001) and his colleagues have made important contributions in designing dynamic assessment techniques for young children, though their approaches tend to be more appropriate for children at the older ages of "early childhood." He and his collaborators have developed the following procedures: The Children's Analogical Thinking Modifiability Test (with Klein), The Children's Inferential Thinking Modifiability Test, The Frame Test of Cognitive Modifiability (with Klein), The Children's Seriational Thinking Modifiability Test, The Complex Figure Test (with Eiboshitz), The Cognitive Modifiability Battery: Assessment and Intervention, The Seria-Think Instrument, and The Children's Conceptual and Perceptual Analogies Test (with Galinka). Tzuriel has also been instrumental in highlighting the importance of noting nonintellective factors (and their modifiability) during the course of the assessment; these include the child's accessibility to mediation, need for mastery, frustration tolerance, locus of control, fear of failure and defensiveness, confidence in correct responses, vitality, and alertness. Tzuriel and his students and colleagues have completed a number of research studies with these instruments. Further information can be obtained from: tzuried@mail.biu.ac.il

For assessors working with very young children, in the infant to toddler range, Kahn's (2000) approach is relevant and elaborated in detail in her chapter. [The only other dynamic approach for this age group of which we are aware is the Syracuse Dynamic Assessment (SDA) by Ensher et al. (1998), described as a play-based procedure designed for use to determine eligibility for intervention services.] Called Dynamic Assessment of Infants' and Toddlers' Abilities (DAITA), Kahn's clinical/descriptive approach focuses on the cognitive actions and motivation for learning of the children, leading to derivation of supportive interventions that optimize their cognitive functioning. DAITA includes a Taxonomy of Cognitive Actions (defined by the author as "mental behaviors that must be activated to perform tasks involving thinking and that can be inferred from observable actions and/or comments" (p. 334)), as well as a Taxonomy of Mediating Learning Strategies ("methods for inducing and creating changes in those [cognitive] actions during dynamic assessment" (p. 334)). The DAITA information can be applied to items the child has failed or refused from any standardized or curriculum-based test; however, Kahn also provides guidelines for applying her approach specifically with the Hawaii Early Learning Profile (VORT, 1995), referring to this as the Dynamic Assessment Approach (DAP). The mediator (parent, assessor, or teacher) is encouraged to re-present items that were failed and that are relevant to the family's goals, making modifications, for example, in materials, time, presentation, response format, until the child is able to respond appropriately. Re-presentations are carried out within the context of the array of cognitive actions and mediating strategies that are relevant to the task.

In the UK, Waters and Stringer (1997) developed The Bunny Bag, a dynamic assessment procedure designed specifically for use by Educational Psychologists (equivalent of School Psychologists in the US) with English children of preschool age. The Bunny Bag, filled with a prescribed list of toys, is a play-based procedure that is used for children with communication problems. A Play Assessment Guide describes developmentally sequenced behaviors to observe for each toy. The assessor provides unstructured mediation/ scaffolding during observation of the interaction of the child with the toys. Information gathered from these observations includes the child's communication, nature of exploration, degree of flexibility and impulsivity, and conditions that promote cognitive development.

There are additional procedures such as Swanson's Cognitive Processing Test (S-CPT; 1995; 2000) in the US, The Learning Potential Test for Ethnic Minorities (LEM; Hamers, Hessels, & Van Luit, 1991; Hessels, 2000) in The Netherlands, and The Analogical Reasoning Learning Test (ARLT; Schlatter & Büchel, 2000) in Switzerland that extend downward to ages five or in the case of the ARLT, even below, but these have not been designed specifically for use with children of preschool age.

It should also be noted that Feuerstein's group in Israel is in the process of adapting their learning potential assessment procedures for application with children of preschool age; however, there is no published information available for this, although training is provided through workshops (see link to the International Center for Evaluation of Learning Potential, ICELP [www.icelp.org].

Dynamic assessment has also been of strong interest to professionals working with children with speech and language disorders, and much of this work is relevant to early childhood. Important contributions in this area have been made by Gutierrez-Clellen, Brown, Robinson-Zañartu, and Conboy (1998), Peña and Gillam (2000), Olswang, Bain, and Johnson (1992), and Tissink (1993). These studies include assessment of phonemic awareness and narrative abilities.

These procedures, their authors, age group, and source are listed in Table 1.

Closing Thoughts And Issues

With increasing emphasis on the ideas of response to intervention and evidence-based instruction and intervention, dynamic assessment has much to offer because this is exactly the type of information available from this approach. Many professionals who find the DA model interesting and of potential relevance and appropriateness find the techniques daunting. Engaging in dynamic assessment does involve and require a paradigm change, and, as we all know, profound change is difficult even for those who are in the business of facilitating change in others. However, the increasingly available literature provides a foundation for professionals to try to cross the threshold. Doing DA is really not all that difficult. Assessors need to change their thinking. The agenda is no longer to pinpoint where the child is at the moment of assessment, but where the child can go with the help of more experienced others. This is what intervention is all about.

Dynamic assessment does not necessarily require more time than traditional approaches. When it does add time, in my view, it is time well spent. It is also not necessary to abandon the procedures with which we have become so comfortable. It is only necessary to understand these tools and to use them appropriately. Metaphors such as "making silk purses out of a sows' ears" or

Table 1: Preschool Dynamic Assessment Procedures

Procedure	Author	Age Range	Source[a]
Curriculum-Based Dynamic Assessment	Lidz	All ages	Lidz (2003)
Application of Cognitive Functions Scale	Lidz & Jepsen	3 to 5	Haywood & Lidz (in preparation) or Lidz at zdilsc@aol.com
Cognitive Modifiability Battery	Tzuriel et al.	4+	tzuried@mail.biu.ac.il
Dynamic Assessment of Infants' and Toddlers' Abilities	Kahn	Infant, toddler	Lidz & Elliott (2000)
The Bunny Bag	Waters & Stringer	Preschool	Waters & Stringer (1997)
The Analogical Reasoning and Learning Test	Schlatter & Buchel	Preschool +	Lidz & Elliott (2000)
Learning Potential Assessment Device for Young Children	Feuerstein et al.	Preschool	International Center for Evaluation of Learning Potential; www.icelp.org
Swanson Cognitive Processing Test	Swanson	5+	ProEd; Austin, TX
The Learning Potential Test for Ethnic Minorities	Hamers, Hessel, & Van Luit	5+	Hamers, Hessel, & Van Luit, 1991; Hessels, 2000

[a] For complete reference, refer to reference list.

"forcing square pegs into round holes" seem to apply. When we need information about how and how well children respond to instruction and directions to explore for subsequent intervention, dynamic assessment offers unique information and holds considerable promise.

Although there has been considerable progress in development of both thinking and procedures since 1983, it is obvious that more needs to be done. There has been much more substantial progress during this time in development of dynamic assessment procedures for use with school age children. The development of preschool procedures has been considerably more modest. Assessment of very young children requires specialized approaches. Downward extensions of measures designed for use with older individuals are not adequate in either administration design or information yielded. Readers are encouraged to use the beginning attempts described in this article to apply their own efforts to development of dynamic assessment procedures for the populations with which they work so that these are carefully molded to the needs of these children and their families. We have come a long way, but we remain early in the journey; the longer road is still ahead.

References

Banks, S. R. & Neisworth, J. T. (1995). Dynamic assessment in early intervention: Implications for serving American Indian/Alaska Native Families. *Journal of American Indian Education, 34(2)*. Online article: http://jaie.asu.edu/v34S2dyn.htm

Burns, M. S., Vye, N. J., Bransford, J. D., Delclos, V., & Ogan, T. (1987). Static and dynamic measures of learning in young handicapped children. *Diagnostique, 12,* 59-73.

Ensher, G. L., Bobish, T. O., Gardner, E. F., Michaels, C. A., Butler, K. G., Foertschi, D. J., et al. (1998). *Syracuse Dynamic Assessment for Birth to Three.* Chicago: Applied Symbolix.

Feuerstein, R., Rand, Y., & Hoffman, M. (1979). *The dynamic assessment of retarded performers: The Learning Potential Assessment Device: Theory, instruments, and techniques.* Baltimore: University Park Press.

Gresham, F. M. (2004). Current status and future directions of school-based behavioral interventions. *School Psychology Review, 33 (3),* 126-343.

Guthke, J., & Wingenfeld, S. (1992). The learning test concept: Origins, state of the art, and trends. In H.C. Haywood & D. Tzuriel (Eds.), *Interactive assessment* (pp. 64-93). Berlin: Springer-Verlag.

Gutierrez-Clellan, V. F., Brown, S., Robinson-Zañartu, C., & Conboy, B. (1998). Modifiability: A dynamic approach to assessing immediate language change. *Journal of Children's Communication Development, 19(2),* 31-43.

Haeussermann, E. (1958). *Developmental potential of preschool children.* New York: Grune & Stratton.

Hamers, J. H. M., Hessels, M. G. P., & Van Luit, L. E. H. (1991). *Leertest voor etnische minderheden: Test en handleiding [The Learning Potential Test for Ethnic Minorities: Test and manua].* Lisse: Swets and Zeitlinger.

Haywood, H. C. & Lidz, C. S. (in preparation). *Dynamic assessment in practice [working title].* Cambridge, UK: Cambridge University Press.

Hessels, M. G. P. (2000). *The Learning Potential Test for Ethnic Minorities (LEM):* A tool for standardized assessment of children in kindergarten and the first years of primary school. In C. S. Lidz & J. G. Elliott (Eds.), *Dynamic assessment: Prevailing models and applications* (pp.109-131). Amsterdam: JAI/Elsevier Science.

Jedrysek, E., Klapper, A., Pope, L., & Wortis, J. (1972). *Psychoeducational evaluation of the preschool child.* New York: Grune and Stratton.

Jitendra, A. K., Rohena-Diaz, E., & Nolet, V. (1998). A dynamic curriculum-based language assessment: Planning instruction for special needs students who are linguistically diverse. *Preventing School Failure, 42 (4),* 182-185.

Kahn, R. J. (2000). Dynamic assessment of infants and toddlers. In C. S. Lidz & J. G. Elliott (Eds.), *Dynamic assessment: Prevailing models and applications* (pp. 325-373). Amsterdam: JAI/Elsevier Science.

Kaufman, A. S., & Kaufman, N. L. (1983). *Kaufman Assessment Battery for Children: Administration and Scoring Manual, and Interpretive Manual.* Circle Pines, MN: American Guidance Service.

Lidz, C. S. (1991). *Practitioner's guide to dynamic assessment.* New York: Guilford.

Lidz, C. S. (2000). The Application of Cognitive Functions Scale: An example of curriculum-based dynamic assessment. In C. S. Lidz & J.G. Elliott (Eds.), *Dynamic assessment: Prevailing models and applications* (pp. 407-439). Amsterdam: JAI/Elsevier Science.

Lidz, C. S. (2001). Multicultural issues and dynamic assessment. In L. A. Suzuki, J. G. Ponterotto, & P. J. Meller (Eds.), *Handbook of Multicultural Assessment: Clinical, Psychological, and Educational Applications, Second Edition* (pp. 523-539). San Francisco: Jossey-Bass.

Lidz, C. S. (2003). *Early childhood assessment.* New York: Wiley.

Lidz, C. S., & Greenberg, K. H. (1997). Criterion validity of a group dynamic assessment procedure with rural first grade regular education students. *Journal of Cognitive Education, 6(2),* 89-99.

Lidz, C. S., Jepsen, R. H., & Miller, M. B. (1997). Relationships between cognitive processes and academic achievement: Application of a group dynamic assessment procedure with multiply handicapped adolescents. *Education and Child Psychology, 14(4),* 56-67.

Lidz, C. S., & Macrine, S. L. (2001). An alternative approach to the identification of gifted culturally and linguistically diverse learners. *School Psychology International, 22(1),* 74-96.

Lidz, C. S., & Thomas, C. (1987). The Preschool Learning Assessment Device: Extension of a static approach. In C. S. Lidz (Ed.), *Dynamic assessment: An interactional approach to evaluating learning potential* (pp. 288-326). New York: Guilford.

Luria, A. R. (1979). *The making of mind-A personal account of Soviet psychology.* Cambridge, MA: Harvard University Press.

Olswang, L., Bain, B., & Johnson, G. (1992). Using dynamic assessment with children with language disorders. In S. Warren & J. Reichle (Eds.), *Causes and effects in communication and language intervention* (pp. 187-216). Baltimore: P.H. Brookes.

Peña, E. (2000). Measurement of modifiability in children from culturally and linguistically diverse backgrounds. *Communication Disorders Quarterly, 2(2),* 87-97.

Peña, E. D., & Gillam, R. B. (2000). Dynamic assessment of children referred for speech and language evaluations. In C. S. Lidz & J. G. Elliott (Eds.), *Dynamic assessment: Prevailing models and applications* (pp. 543-575). Amsterdam: JAI/Elsevier Science.

Reinharth, B. (1989). *Cognitive modifiability of developmentally delayed children.* Unpublished doctoral dissertation, Yeshiva University, New York.

Robinson-Zañartu, C. (1996). Serving Native American children and families: Considering cultural variables. *Language, Speech, and Hearing Services in Schools, 27(4),* 373-384.

Schlatter, C., & Büchel, F. P. (2000). Detecting reasoning abilities of persons with moderate mental retardation: *The Analogical Reasoning Learning Test (ARLT).* In C. S. Lidz & J. G. Elliott (Eds.), *Dynamic assessment: Prevailing models and applications* (pp. 155-186). Amsterdam: JAI/Elsevier Science.

Siegler, R. S. (1983). Information processing approaches to development. In P. Mussen (Ed.), *Handbook of child psychology (4th ed.). Volume I: History, theory, and methods* (pp. 129-211). New York: Wiley.

Spector, J. E. (1992). Predicting progress in beginning reading: Dynamic assessment of phonemic awareness. *Journal of Educational Psychology, 84,* 353-363.

Sternberg, R. J., Grigorenko, E. L., Ngorosho, D., Tantufuye, E., Mbise, A., Nokes, C., et al. (2002). Assessing intellectual potential in rural Tarzanian school children. *Intelligence, 30(2),* 141-162.

Swanson, H. L. (1995). *Swanson-Cognitive Processing Test.* Austin, TX: PRO-ED.

Swanson, H. S. (2000). *Swanson-Cognitive Processing Test:* Review and applications. In C. S. Lidz & J. G. Elliott (Eds.), *Dynamic assessment: Prevailing models and applications* (pp. 71-107). Amsterdam: JAI/Elsevier Science.

Tissink, J. (1993). De constructie van leertests met curriculum(on)gebonden taken [The construction of learning tests with curriculum (un)related tasks]. Utrecht: ISOR, PhD thesis.

Tzuriel, D. (2001). *Dynamic assessment of young children.* New York: Kluwer Academic/Plenum.

VORT (1995). *HELP for Preschoolers (3-6).* Palo Alto, CA: Author.

Waters, J., & Stringer, P. (1997). The Bunny Bag: A dynamic approach to the assessment of preschool children. *Educational and Child Psychology, 14(4),* 33-45.

The Reliability and Discriminant Validity of the Social Interactive Coding System with Language Delayed Preschoolers

MaryAnne Picone
Geneva City School District

Paul C. McCabe
Brooklyn College – City University of New York

The Social Interactive Coding System (SICS) is designed to examine the social interaction patterns of language impaired preschoolers in a school setting. Administrators of the SICS code who the target child is speaking with, their interactions, where in the classroom they are playing, and the quality of their play. This study examined the internal consistency and test-retest stability of the SICS over three assessment intervals six to eight weeks apart. Also, this study examined the discriminant validity of the SICS as a method to differentiate between language impaired and non-impaired peers. Results indicated that several categories on the SICS were particularly sensitive in discriminating between language impaired and non-impaired peers, including whether the child preferred addressing adults versus peers, the length of the typical verbal response, and the quality of their play. Test-retest and internal consistency coefficients were low to moderate. Limitations including sample size, test-retest interval, and specific restrictions of the SICS were addressed, and directions for future research were provided.

MaryAnne Picone, Geneva Central School District, Geneva, NY; Paul C. McCabe, Graduate Program in School Psychology, Brooklyn College, City University of New York, New York. Correspondence concerning this article should be addressed to Paul C. McCabe, Graduate Program in School Psychology, Brooklyn College – CUNY, 2900 Bedford Ave., Brooklyn, NY 11210. Electronic mail may be sent to: PaulMc@brooklyn.cuny.edu

Both language and social interaction skills have been considered important components of definitions of social competence. Researchers have argued that language and communication ability play a critical role in one's social interaction success and overall social competence (Gallagher, 1993; McCabe & Meller, 2004). The importance of social competence as a developmental construct is well established, including numerous studies indicating that socially competent children enjoy social, academic, and occupational successes later in life, while those children exhibiting deficiencies of socially competent behaviors tend to have much poorer outcomes (Denham et al., 2003; Elias, Gara, Schuyler, Brandon-Muller, & Sayette, 1991).

There are numerous ways to assess a child's social competence. Some researchers have advocated for assessment of social competence within a naturalistic environment to best capture the nuances and subtleties of social interactions that may be overlooked by more laboratory-based assessments (McCabe, 2005; Merrell, 2001). Within the natural context, social competence has been directly observed through clique analysis (Storey & Smith, 1995), peer relationships and acceptance (Asher, 1990), language ability (Gertner & Rice, 1994), and social interactions (Girolametto & Weitzman, 2002). Coding systems can be a beneficial way to assess a child's language ability and social interactions. One such system, the Social Interactive Coding System, was designed to systematically code the verbal communications between preschoolers within a social context (Rice, Sell, & Hadley, 1990). Although the system appears promising for use in both typical preschools as well as those serving children with specific language impairments (SLI), there have not been independent validation studies to confirm its utility. The purpose of this study is to determine the test-retest stability, internal consistency, and discriminant validity of this instrument with typical and SLI preschool children.

When a child is considered socially competent, they are generally capable of using language and verbal skills to make appropriate social choices when confronted with a range of situational choices (Brown & Bergen, 2002). They also socially participate and interact with peers. Indeed, social competence is reflected more in the quality than the frequency of children's social interactions (Wright, 1980). Many situational factors influence a child's participation, peer interaction, and use of language and verbal skills. These include: playmate familiarity, types of toys they use, activities they engage in, presence of adults, extent to which teachers adopt a directive role, and characteristics of children's playmates. The ability to gain the attention of peers and lead peers in play, to use appropriate strategies to enter existing play groups, to utilize peers as resources, and to show affection are all individual social behaviors that support the development of social competence (Guralnick & Groom, 1985).

Language is used to make interpersonal contact, form relationships, and regulate our interactions (Gallagher, 1993). Children who are SLI typically appear and respond differently than their non-language impaired (NLI) peers. SLI children have a history of social interaction failures that result from their communication impairment. As they endure repeated social failures, they often choose to not interact with their peers and withdraw from social situations. They also may ignore or fail to respond to the social initiations of peers and adults. SLI children are more likely to use parallel play with their peers. To make matters worse, NLI children do not always accept SLI children (Shirin & Kreimeyer, 1996). Fantasy, dramatic play is highly verbally demanding, and therefore SLI children are at risk for peer rejection due to their inability or difficulty in participation when engaged in interactive play scenarios (Gallagher, 1993). It has been suggested that a lack of confidence in language ability leads to a delay in social competence (Halle, 1985).

It is therefore important that assessment of social competence include an examination of a child's efficacy in social communication. Unfortunately, most measures of social competence do not include response sets that directly address the verbal component of social interaction successes and failures. A direct observation of these skills *in vivo* is currently the only way to reliably assess a child's social communicative success. Observation coding systems are used for recording the behaviors of individuals, identifying their antecedents and sequelae, recording the interactions between children, adults, activities and materials, and recording the sequence of events in a particular setting while a child is performing a task (Bramlett & Barnett, 1993). This information can then be applied to specific curricula and activities. The use of direct observation is also very practical, particularly in preschool settings, and especially during playtime and playground time (Merrell, 2001).

The Social Interactive Coding System (SICS) was developed to record the social interactions of language impaired students in the authors' Language Acquisition Preschool (Rice et al., 1990). The SICS is designed to record continuous verbal interactions as a function of play areas, addressees, script coders, and play levels. Their original goal was to create a coding system that "produced clinically useful, reliable information about children's uses of language in classroom contexts, with a minimum of time demands, specialized training, or specialized equipment" (Rice et al., 1990, p. 2). The coding system was designed to measure situational variables that may influence social interactions. Observations were made during a 40-minute free playtime that was included as part of daily activities. Free play time included allowing the children to play freely in any of the four areas in the classroom that were available: quiet area, the block area, the art table, and the dramatic play area. The SICS was used to follow a target child's interactions throughout the course of a day.

Rice et al.'s (1990) findings suggest that the data sheets are easily under-stood when used to explain an individual's social interaction pattern. The SICS can also be used to determine an individual child's preferential play area or activ-ity. This can be helpful in determining reinforcing events for a child. It also records who the child interacted with and who initiated the conversation. The instrument is also beneficial in that it has space to record the play level. For example, the child is recorded as playing alone, alongside another child, or inte-grated play with one or more children.

Rice et al. (1991) demonstrated the efficacy of the SICS in distinguishing among the language and social behaviors of typical, SLI, and English as a sec-ond language (ESL) preschoolers. The typically developing preschoolers tended to initiate more with peers, and had longer responses. Other typically-developing peers were the preferred addressees. SLI children were likely to initiate with adults versus peers, and had shorter responses or more nonverbal responses. ESL children tended to be least likely to initiate and were also least chosen as addressees.

The utility of the SICS in assessing the language and social interaction behaviors of typical and SLI preschoolers has not been verified and confirmed beyond Rice et al.'s original studies. The purpose of this study was to determine whether the SICS was able to differentiate between the social interactions of lan-guage impaired and non-language impaired preschoolers in an independent sample. The internal consistency was examined using reliability analysis, and stability was measured through correlational analysis. It was hypothesized that all categories of the SICS would remain stable over three subsequent intervals, although some change due to maturation was expected. It was also hypothesized that the SICS would successfully differentiate between SLI and NLI preschool-ers, particularly in the categories of Addressee, Verbal Interactive Status and the Play Level, based on Rice et al.'s (1991) previous findings.

Method

Participants

Fifty-nine children enrolled in preschool programs served as participants in this study upon receipt of parental consent. To be included as a participant, the children needed to be assessed three different times over a six month period (every two months). Of the initial 59 participants, a total of 13 children did not complete the study. Reasons for not completing the study included families moving out of the area, children switching daycare facilities, and summer vaca-tion when children did not attend daycare. Thus, 46 children were included in the final sample. Thirty children were classified specific language impaired (SLI) and 16 were non-language impaired (NLI).

The samples of SLI children were enrolled in one self-contained and three integrated classrooms that specialized in the education and remediation of preschoolers with language impairment. The classrooms were operated by a private, non-profit speech and hearing clinic in a medium-sized metropolitan area. Two certified speech-language pathologists and a classroom aide taught these students. The age range of the SLI group was 3 years, 5 months to 5 years, 1 month (mean age = 4 years, 2 months). Out of the 30 children, 27 were males and 3 were females. The ratio of SLI males to females is higher than the reported prevalence rates of between 2:1 and 3:1 male-to-female ratio (Choudhury & Benasich, 2003). The racial makeup included 21 Caucasians, 5 African Americans, 3 Latinos, and 1 other representation. English was identified as the primary language for all children participating in the study. The three integrated settings served a suburban and urban population. Low, middle, and upper-middle class families were represented equally in the integrated SLI sample population. In the self-contained setting, a higher distribution of low and middle-income families from an urban setting was served. The average income for the SLI family sample was $30-45,000/year.

Determination of SLI classroom eligibility was based on the decision of the child's district Committee on Preschool Special Education following New York State guidelines. The children enrolled in the SLI classrooms were required to be of preschool age (3-5 years) and have met the following criteria: 1) educational classification of developmental delay in the functional area of communication; 2) communication delay was the primary area of delay versus a cognitive, motor, or other developmental disorder; and 3) if children had delays in other areas, these delays were secondary to, or intertwined with, their communication delay. For instance, some children had verbal cognitive delays with average nonverbal cognitive skills, or fine motor delays related to their speech impediment (e.g., oral motor weakness or dyspraxia).

The samples of NLI children were recruited from two full day preschool programs through a daycare facility. One of these facilities housed one of the integrated SLI classrooms mentioned above. There was a teacher and a classroom aide who taught the students in each classroom. The age range of the NLI group was 3 years, 0 months to 5 years, 0 months (mean age = 4 years, 3 months). Out of 16 children 8 were males and 8 were females. The racial makeup included 14 Caucasians, 1 Latino, and 1 Asian. Both facilities served a suburban and urban population. Low, middle, and upper-middle class families were represented equally in the NLI sample population. The average income for the NLI family sample was $30-45,000/year.

NLI status was determined by requiring the children to be of preschool age (3-5 years) and meeting the following criteria: 1) having never been referred for speech/language evaluation; 2) teachers did not report any concerns regarding the children's current level of speech/language functioning; 3) speech language pathologists, when working with the SLI children during integration periods, did not observe any deficiencies in speech or language functioning in the non-impaired children; 4) independent observations by licensed psychologists specially trained in the assessment of speech-language impairments did not raise any further concerns regarding their speech/language development; and 5) the child's physician did not report any concerns regarding the children's current level of speech/language functioning.

Procedure

Parents were explained the purpose of the study through a letter, which also asked them to sign and return the attached informed consent. Upon receipt of parental consent, the children were observed in their preschool during free play times during which the children played in one of five centers in the classroom: Build and Pretend, Cut and Create, Move and Groove, Touch and Explore, and Sound Town. These centers were similar to those in the original study (Rice et al., 1990). Build and Pretend was an area that included toys which encourage the use of imagination and social interactive playing, such as blocks, dollhouses, Lego's, and baby dolls. Cut and Create was a craft area where the children made various types of art projects. Move and Groove was a play center where the children played interactive games. Touch and Explore was a sensory play area, usually either a sand table or a water table. Sound Town was the quietest area, where children could read or listen to a story. Each child was observed for 5 consecutive minutes on three different days, during different times of day whenever possible. Although the SICS authors proposed observations be completed on the same day during the same free play, it was hypothesized that this may not give the most accurate picture of the child (see Doll & Elliot, 1994). Thus, observations were completed over 2-3 weeks to achieve a more accurate reflection of each child's social behavior. Observers did not interact with the children; rather, they positioned themselves far enough away from the play area to be unobtrusive, yet close enough to hear the children speaking. Each child was observed for three 5-minute intervals, conducted over a one-week period, thus equaling fifteen minutes per assessment period. The three assessment periods were separated by six-eight week intervals. In total, each child was observed for forty-five minutes during the 6-month study.

SICS training. Two graduate school psychology students were trained in the Social Interactive Coding System (SICS) according to the procedures outlined by Rice and colleagues (1990) and were supervised by a licensed psychologist with expertise in the assessment and treatment of specific language impairment in preschool children. Five videotaped sessions were taken by the observers to use as a training system. During these sessions, children were videotaped for five minutes each. Next, the observers reviewed each video session and coded social interactions independently. Discrepancies were discussed while the observers reviewed the taped intervals. Training to use the SICS and the four videotaped sessions took approximately 9 hours.

Inter-rater reliability was measured using the fifth videotaped session. Reliability was found by calculating the percent of agreement between raters on each separate category of the SICS. This was done by dividing the number of agreements by the total number of occurrences for each category. The percent agreement on the number of interactions coded by both observers was 98%. Most of the discrepancies occurred because of videotape limitations. This included limited viewing perspective and the inability to hear each student clearly. The second set of reliabilities was determined by each category and used the interactions coded from both observers. The percent agreements were as follows: play activity, 100%; addressee, 97%; verbal interactive status, 91%; script code, 100%; and play level, 100%. The overall reliability was 98%.

After reliability was established with the videotapes, both observers collected data simultaneously in the classroom coding the same target student. The percent agreement on the number of interactions coded by both observers through live coding was 96%. Most discrepancies occurred due to obstruction or partial obstruction of view of one of the observers. This happened when the target child moved quickly from one play area to another or was continuously moving about the room throughout the coding time. The percent agreements for each category were as follows: play activity, 100%; addressee, 96%; verbal interactive status, 89%; script code, 100%; and play level, 95%.

The inter-rater reliabilities upon completion of training were satisfactory according to the procedures outlined by Rice et al. (1990), and therefore each rater was able to complete subsequent observations independently. To ensure adherence to observation protocol, inter-rater reliability checks occurred at the beginning of the two follow-up assessment periods, roughly 6 weeks and 12 weeks after the initial training. The overall inter-rater reliability agreements for those periods were 94% and 97%, respectively.

SICS administration. The SICS protocol permitted a target child's verbal and social interactions to be coded for a specific amount of time. Other variables that were coded included play activity, addressee, verbal interactive status, script codes, and play level. These are described in more detail below. The time at the beginning and end of each coding segment was recorded. Each coding segment was 5-minutes, during which all the target child's interactions were coded. After each segment, the observer took a 5-minute break. This break in coding was designed to maximize the level of concentration during coding segments, as well as enable the observer to fill in any codes that may have been missed during the observation.

The variable of *play activity* refers to the numerous possible play areas accessible to the children. There were five possible areas in the classrooms: Build and Pretend, Touch and Explore, Cut and Create, Sound Town, and Move and Grove.

The variable *addressee* refers to the person whom the child is speaking or interacting with. There are three possible subcategories under this variable. The child can either be conversing with an adult or children in the classroom. The third option is coded as general. In this subcategory, a child initiates an interaction to no particular person. The addressee variable is then calculated as the grand total of all interactions divided by those interactions with either a child, adult, or general. This is a continuous variable, ranging from 0 to 1.

The *verbal interactive status* (VIS) category is designated for interactions that include initiations, responses or ignores. These subcategories code whether the target child initiates an interaction, repeats an initiation, ignores an initiation from an addressee, responds verbally with one word response, responds verbally with two words, responds verbally with multiple words, or responds nonverbally and continues the interaction. Each line on the data sheet represents the target child's turn of the interaction. At the end of each interaction, an X is marked. This allows interactions to be briefly viewed to see the child's typical interaction pattern. The subcategories are calculated as the grand total of all initiations and/or responses divided by the number of initiations, repeats, ignores, one-word responses, etc. Thus, each subcategory is a continuous variable, ranging from 0 to 1. The category Total Verbal Interactive Status (VIS) was the sum of all initiations, responses, or ignores, and is a continuous whole number.

The variable *script code* refers to the specific activity the child is doing within the play area. There are six subcategories for script codes. The first is dramatic play where a child is participating in play with a dramatic theme. The second a project where a child was doing an art project or building with manipulatives or blocks. The third is the quiet area, where children were either looking at books or completing puzzles. The fourth code was games where a child was playing a game directed by the speech pathologist, classroom teacher, or classroom aide. The fifth code was wandering. This code was used when the child was wandering around the room with no directed focus to a particular play area. Finally there was the looking-around code. This was used when a child was sitting observing activities around the room instead of engaging in play. The subcategories are calculated by dividing the grand total of all script codes by the specific activity (dramatic play, project, etc.), yielding a continuous variable ranging from 0 to 1.

The last variable was *play level*. The focus of this variable was to determine the child's relationship to other students in the class. If a child was interacting with adults only, the corresponding column on the record form was left blank. If the child was alone in a play area for one minute or longer then the solitary play code was used. If the child was in a play area with one or more other children but was not playing with them the adjacent play code was used. The final code was social interactive play. This code was used when the target child and other children were playing together with one object, game or were involved in one pretend play theme. The subcategories were calculated by dividing the grand total of play status by the specific play types observed (solitary, adjacent, social interactive, or a combination), thus generating a continuous variable ranging from 0 to 1.

Results

Stability of the SICS

Temporal stability was explored using Pearson product-moment correlations to analyze the data from the first data collection to the second, the second data collection to the third, and the first data collection to the third. Table 1 presents the test-retest reliability as Pearson-product moment correlations. For stability from the first data collection to the second data collection, the following categories were significant: Child, r (46) = .46, $p < .01$; Adult, r (46) = .42, $p < .01$; Multiple Word Response, r (46) = .34, $p < .05$; Nonverbal Response, r (46) = .30, $p < .05$; Total Verbal Interactive Status, r (46) = .29, $p < .05$; and Social Interactive Play Level, r (46) = .48, $p < .01$. The following categories were significant from the second data collection to the third data collection: Adult, r (47) = .40, $p < 0.01$; Multiple Word Response, r (47) = .32, $p < .05$; and Adjacent Play Level, r (47) = .30, $p < .05$. The following categories were significant from first data collection to the third data collection: Multiple Word Responses, r (47) = .37, $p < .05$; Nonverbal Response, r (47) = .33, $p < .05$; Total Interactive Status, r (47) = .43, $p < .01$; and Social Interactive Play Level, r (47) = .36, $p < .05$.

Internal consistency reliability estimates were obtained for the SICS categories by collapsing all three assessment periods and obtaining an average alpha coefficient. The alpha coefficients are provided in Table 1. Moderate alpha coefficients were obtained for Child Addressee (.56), Adult Addressee (.63), Multiple Word Response (.60), Nonverbal Response (.38), Total Verbal Interactive Status (.55), Adjacent Play Level (.45), and Social Interactive Play Level (.49). Low internal consistency was found in the remaining SICS categories.

Table 1: Test-retest stability (Pearson-product moment correlations) and internal consistency (alpha coefficients, averaged across the three time intervals) of the Social Interactive Coding System for entire sample

SICS Category	Test-retest interval (r values)			Alpha
Addressee	$1^{st} - 2^{nd}$	$2^{nd} - 3^{rd}$	$1^{st} - 3^{rd}$	
Child	.46**	.21	.24	.56
Adult	.42**	.40**	.27	.63
General	-.03	.02	.25	.18
Verbal Interactive Status				
Initiations	.05	-.05	.25	.16
Repeat	-.11	.28	.03	.20
One Word Response	-.19	.22	-.18	.10
Two Word Response	-.15	.03	.03	.10
Multiple Word Response	.34*	.32*	.37*	.60
Nonverbal Response	.30*	.18	.33*	.38
Ignore	.27	-.11	-.04	.22
Total VIS	.29*	.17	.43**	.55
Play Level				
Solitary	.23	.15	.09	.35
Adjacent	.27	.30*	.06	.45
Social Interactive	.48**	.04	.36*	.49

* $p < .05$
** $p < .01$

Discriminant validity of the SIC

A one-way repeated measures analysis of variance (ANOVA) was used to examine whether the SICS variables were able to discriminate between SLI and NLI groups across the three assessment periods. Each SICS variable was entered as a separate within-subjects factor. The SICS was able to successfully discriminate between SLI and NLI groups on the following categories: Child Addressee, $F(1, 44) = 94.38$, $p < .001$, partial eta^2 = .68; Adult Addressee, $F(1, 44) = 40.89$, $p < .001$, partial eta^2 = .48; Multiple Word Response, $F(1, 44) = 48.62$, $p < .001$, partial eta^2 = .53; Nonverbal Response, $F(1, 44) = 7.91$, $p < .01$, partial eta^2 = .15; Ignoring, $F(1, 44) = 4.47$, $p < .001$, partial eta^2 = .09; Adjacent Play Level, $F(1, 44) = 15.45$, $p < .001$, partial eta^2 = .26; and Social Interactive Play Level, $F(1, 44) = 29.06$, $p < .001$, partial eta^2 = .40. An analysis of mean scores across the three assessment periods indicated that NLI children were more than twice as likely to engage a child addressee (.57 vs. .24) and use multiple word responses (.31 vs. 15), and four times as likely to engage in social interactive play (.23 vs. .05). SLI children, on the other hand, were more likely to engage an adult addressee (.66 vs. .37), use nonverbal responses to a verbal initiation by a peer or adult (.19 vs. .12), ignore a verbal initiation (.06 vs. .03), and engage in adjacent play (.74 vs. .55). The results of the ANOVA are presented in Table 2.

Discussion

The purpose of this study was to provide an independent examination of the stability and reliability of the SICS in determining its utility for recording the social interactions of preschoolers with specific language impairment. The SICS was also examined for its ability to successfully differentiate between the social and communicative behaviors of SLI children and NLI children.

Between group analysis indicated that the SICS successfully differentiated between SLI children and NLI children on several variables. The SLI group conversed more frequently with adults, and less frequently with their peers. It was noticed that the NLI children often did not respond to the initiations of SLI children, and therefore the SLI children tended to direct their verbalizations toward adults. SLI children may be drawn to adults because they are more likely to respond if the child initiates a social interaction. These results confirm those of Rice et al. (1991).

Another finding was that the SLI group ignored the initiations of their peers more often than NLI group. SLI children are often quiet, withdrawn, and ignore the initiations and responses of adults and other children. Because SLI children

Table 2: Repeated-measures analysis of variance (ANOVA) of SICS variables across 3 assessment periods (1st, 2nd, and 3rd) by language status (NLI vs. SLI).

SICS Category	M^1	SD^1	M^2	SD^2	F	p	Eta-squared
Addressee							
Child	.24	.10	.57	.12	94.38	.000	.68
Adult	.66	.16	.37	.11	40.89	.000	.48
General	.07	.05	.06	.06	0.57	.456	.01
Verbal Interactive Status							
Initiations	.29	.09	.31	.11	0.47	.497	.01
Repeat	.04	.03	.03	.02	1.78	.189	.04
One Word Response	.19	.08	.14	.06	3.69	.061	.08
Two Word Response	.05	.03	.05	.03	0.21	.647	.01
Multiple Word Response	.15	.08	.31	.07	48.62	.000	.53
Nonverbal Response	.19	.10	.12	.05	7.91	.007	.15
Ignore	.06	.04	.03	.02	4.47	.040	.09
Total VIS	26.23	10.00	29.00	8.90	0.86	.360	.02
Play Level							
Solitary	.18	.14	.21	.15	0.40	.530	.01
Adjacent	.74	.16	.55	.14	15.45	.000	.26
Social Interaction	.05	.06	.23	.16	29.06	.000	.40

Note: df = 1, 44
[1] = SLI group, [2] = NLI group

do not socially interact with others as often as NLI children, they may simply be unaware of the initiations made. SLI children also used less multiple-word responses, perhaps due to their delays in speech and language. Instead, they were more likely to respond with one or two word responses or with nonverbal responses, such as pointing and head nodding. Finally, SLI children played alongside peers, regardless of the peers' speech and language ability, and were less likely to engage in social interactive play than their non-impaired counterparts. These results mirror those obtained by Rice et al. (1991) and suggest that the SICS demonstrates adequate discriminant validity for parsing behaviors idiosyncratic to SLI children from their non-impaired counterparts.

Conversely, the NLI children played and interacted more with their NLI peers than their SLI peers. NLI children tended to have the social and speech/language abilities they needed to appear comfortable socially interacting with other peers their age. In general, this NLI group was more aware of social interactions. They did not ignore the adults and peers who were interacting with them. They also used their words to describe how they felt, asked for something they wanted or needed, and interacted more often with peers as well as adults. NLI children actively engaged in play with other NLI children, but did not interact as frequently with the SLI children. SLI children played more alongside another child, but they typically did not interact with the child. The NLI children not only played more often with other children, but they also tended to direct their verbalizations toward their peers. This reciprocal dynamic underscores how socialization and communication are fostered through interactive play, and how SLI children are at-risk for ongoing socialization difficulties because they lack the opportunities and initiative of their non-impaired peers.

The analysis of the test-retest stability of the SICS indicated that some categories were much better at discriminating among the SLI and NLI categories, both initially and over time. Other categories on the SICS were not helpful in discriminating groups and also did not score consistently across assessment intervals. The multiple-word response category was the only code that was stable over all three data collections. Therefore, it consistently measured multiword responses between the two groups independent of the child's language ability. The total verbal interactive status, social interactive play level, and adult interactions with the target student were also stable; however they were only statistically significant over 2 data collections. Child addressee and adjacent play level were only stable over one time interval. Internal consistency reliabilities mirrored the test-retest findings, with child addressee, adult addressee, multiple-word responses, nonverbal responses, total verbal interactive status, adjacent play level, and social interactive play level showing moderate stability, and the remaining categories showing low stability.

Stability and reliability of coding systems, designed for young children, are difficult to evaluate. This is due to a child's continuously changing ability and functioning levels. Researchers have investigated the most reliable intervals for observing preschoolers, and have argued that approximately three weeks should be the maximum amount of time between data collections (Merrell, 2001). It is possible that the test-retest reliabilities would have been somewhat higher if a shorter interval was used in this study. The present results suggest that the SICS may be useful for evaluating brief, intensive intervention programs, but may be less useful as a long-term, pretest-posttest or progress-monitoring measure (e.g., September to June intervals).

Some codes on the SICS were neither stable, reliable, nor could they successfully differentiate between the SLI children and the NLI children. There should be some consideration of revising the SICS and eliminating the codes that were not statistically sound or did not produce meaningful data. Examples of these types of codes are the General Addressee, One Word Response, and Two Word Response. These codes may be more meaningful for younger toddlers who are just beginning to communicate. Reducing the number of non-meaningful or unreliable codes will allow observers more opportunity to accurately record the more relevant categories.

There were several limitations to this study. The first limitation was attrition. A total of thirteen children did not complete the study. Reasons included families moving out of the area, children switching day care facilities, and summer vacation. While it is unlikely that those children who left the study prematurely are characteristically different than those who remained, it is possible that social interactive status could be slightly different due to varying exposure to peers. Another limitation related to sample size was inequity of students in the SLI and NLI groups. More students that participated in the SLI category were available all three assessment periods than those in the NLI category. In addition, the SLI group had significantly more males than females. The representation of males to females was higher than the established prevalence rate.

Another limitation was encountered as the coders attempted to record verbal interactions. There were times when a child would speak too softly or turn his/her back and the observer could not hear the individual. Because live coders were used, interactions could not be replayed. The coders also did not want to be intrusive during observation settings and influence the social interactions of the children; however, it became difficult to see and hear if the child was speaking.

The last limitations were those directly related to the SICS. First, the SICS does not record the individual utterances provided by each target child. Second, there is no record of what the addressee did to initiate or invite an interaction with the target child. It also does not track the duration of interaction. There is only one continuous reference to the elapsed time. Finally the SICS is limited to one conversational dimension; that is, one of assertion (initiations) or passivity (responses). These are then divided further into subcategories with a very rough indication of length of interaction.

The SICS appears to be a moderately reliable and valid tool when used to discriminate the social and verbal behaviors between SLI and NLI children. It may also be effective in tracking changes in social interactive status over short intervals. Further research is needed to focus on various coding systems that provide authentic, real-time assessment, particularly in early childhood when maturational changes are abundant. Numerous systems have been designed based on theories of development but lack the empirical support for continued use. Research should also focus on the construction of other coding systems that could be used with SLI children, particularly in light of recent evidence highlighting the high comorbidity between specific language impairment and social and behavioral dysfunction.

References

Asher, S. R. (1990). Recent advances in the study of peer rejection. In S.R. Asher & J.D. Cole (Eds.), *Peer rejection in childhood* (pp. 3-14). Cambridge: Cambridge University Press.

Bramlett, R. K. & Barnett, D. W. (1993). The development of a direct observation code for use in preschool settings. *School Psychology Review, 22(1),* 49-62.

Brown, M., & Bergen, D. (2002). Play and social interactions of children with disabilities at learning/activity centers in an inclusive preschool. *Journal of Research in Childhood Education, 17(1),* 26-37.

Choudhury, N., & Benasich, A. (2003). The influence of family history and other risk factors on language development. *Journal of Speech, Language, and Hearing Research, 46,* 261-272.

Denham, S. A., Blair, K. A., DeMulder, E., Levitas, J., Sawyer, K., Auerbach-Major, S. et al. (2003). Preschool emotional competence: Pathway to social competence? *Child Development, 74(1),* 238-256.

Doll, B., & Elliot, S. N. (1994). Research methods: Representativeness of observed preschool social behaviors: How many data are enough? *Journal of Early Intervention, 18(2),* 227-238.

Elias, M. J., Gara, M. A., Schuyler, T. F., Branden-Muller, L. R., & Sayette, M. A. (1991). The promotion of social competence: Longitudinal study of preventive school-based program. *American Journal of Orthopsychiatry, 61*, 409-417.

Gallagher, T. M. (1993). Language skills and the development of social competence in school age children. *Language, Speech, and Hearing Services in Schools, 24*, 199-205.

Gertner, B. L., & Rice, M. L. (1994). Influence of communicative competence on peer preferences in a preschool classroom. *Journal of Speech & Hearing Research, 37(4),* 913-924.

Girolametto, L., & Weitzman, E. (2002). Responsiveness of child care providers in interactions with toddlers and preschoolers. *Language, Speech, and Hearing Services in Schools, 33*, 268-281.

Guralnick, M. J., & Groom, J. M. (1985). Correlates of peer-related social competence of developmentally delayed preschool children. *American Association on Mental Deficiencies, 90(2),* 140-150.

Halle, J. W. (1985). Enhancing social competence through language: An experimental analysis of a practical procedure for teachers. *Topics in Early Childhood Special Education, 4(4),* 77-92.

McCabe, P. C., & Meller, P. J. (2004). The relationship between language and social competence: How language delays affect social growth. *Psychology in the Schools, 41(3),* 313-312.

McCabe, P. C. (2005). Social and behavioral correlates of preschoolers with specific language impairment. *Psychology in the Schools, 42(4),* 1-15.

Merrell, K. W. (2001). Assessment of children's social skills: Recent development, best practices, and new directions. *Exceptionality, 9(1),* 3-19.

Rice, M. L., Sell, M. A., & Hadley, P. A. (1990). The social interactive coding system (SICS): an on-line, clinically relevant descriptive tool. *Language, Speech, and Hearing Services in Schools, 21*, 2-14.

Rice, M. L., Sell, M. A., & Hadley, P. A. (1991). Social interactions of speech and language impaired children. *Journal of Speech and Hearing Research, 34*, 1299-1307.

Shirin, S. D., & Kreimeyer, K. H. (1996). Social interaction and acceptance of deaf or hard-of-hearing children and their peers: A comparison of social-skills and familiarity-based interventions. *Volta Review, 98(4),*157-181.

Storey, K., & Smith, D. J. (1995). Assessing integration in early childhood education: Clique analysis of social interactions. *Education & Treatment of Children, 18(2),* 158-184.

Wright, M. J. (1980). Measuring the social competence of preschool children. *Canadian Journal of Behavioral Science, 12*, 17-32.

www.ingramcontent.com/pod-product-compliance
Lightning Source LLC
Chambersburg PA
CBHW020005290326
41935CB00007B/309